ALICE

Laura Wade

ALICE

An adaptation of Lewis Carroll's
Alice In Wonderland

OBERON BOOKS
LONDON

First published in 2010 by Oberon Books Ltd
521 Caledonian Road, London N7 9RH
Tel: +44 (0) 20 7607 3637 / Fax: +44 (0) 20 7607 3629
e-mail: info@oberonbooks.com
www.oberonbooks.com

A catalogue record for this book is available from the
British Library.

PB ISBN: 978-1-84943-067-8
E ISBN: 978-1-84943-357-0

Cover photograph of Ruby Bentall by Craig Fleming
www.craig-fleming.com

Cover design by Rare Company

Printed and bound by CPI Group (UK) Ltd, Croydon, CR0 4YY.

Acknowledgements

Alice grew out of a close writer-director collaboration, therefore my biggest thanks go to Lyndsey Turner, the best friend a new play could have.

We'd both like to thank the following people and organisations who helped with the development of the play: The National Theatre Studio, The Actors' Centre, Samuel West and in particular, Daniel Evans and the staff of Sheffield Theatres.

LW June 2010

Characters

SHEFFIELD

ALICE

CATERING WOMAN

MUM

DAD

GRANDDAD

AUNTIE

UNCLE

TEACHER

TOM

DAN

WAITER

COUSIN

LEN

JIM

TWO LITTLE BOYS

LITTLE GIRL

JOE

FUNERAL GUESTS

WONDERLAND

WHITE RABBIT

CATERPILLAR

POSTMAN

COOK

DUCHESS

CHESHIRE CAT

HATTER

HARE

DORMOUSE

BOY

GIRL

KNAVE OF HEARTS

TWO CROQUET COMMENTATORS

FLAMINGO

HEDGEHOG

QUEEN OF HEARTS

KING OF HEARTS

CROQUET OFFICIAL

HUMPTY DUMPTY

MOCK TURTLE

GRYPHON

LOBSTERS

TWEEDLEDUM

TWEEDLEDEE

COURT OFFICIAL

Note:

The following Sheffield/Wonderland characters should be
doubled by the same actor:

MUM – QUEEN
DAD – KING
AUNTIE – DUCHESS – MOCK TURTLE
TEACHER – HUMPTY DUMPTY
TOM AND DAN – TWEEDLEDUM AND TWEEDLEDEE
COUSIN – CHESHIRE CAT
LEN – HATTER

Other doubling is at the director's discretion.

Alice was first presented by Sheffield Theatres at the Crucible Theatre on 17th June 2010.

Cast

WHITE RABBIT/JOE/WONDERBAND, Jack Beale

ALICE, Ruby Bentall

TWEEDLEDEE/COMMENTATOR/DAN/WONDERBAND, John Biddle

TWEEDLEDUM/COMMENTATOR/TOM/WONDERBAND, Oliver Birch

DUCHESS/MOCK TURTLE/AUNTIE, Beatie Edney

QUEEN/MUM, Pippa Haywood

HUMPTY/GRYPHON/HARE/TEACHER, John Marquez

KING/DAD/DORMOUSE/POSTMAN, Jonathan McGuinness

KNAVE/CHESHIRE CAT/COUSIN/WONDERBAND, Graham O'Mara

HATTER/CATERPILLAR/OFFICIAL/LEN, Graham Turner

Director, Lyndsey Turner

Designer, Naomi Wilkinson

Lighting Designer, Chris Davey

Sound Designer, Christopher Shutt

Movement Director, Aline David

Original Music by David Shrubsole

Alice was developed with the support of the National Theatre Studio.

ACT ONE

The living room of a large Victorian house in Broomhill – the home of the Little family, currently hosting a post-funeral tea on a November afternoon.

ALICE sits in the centre of the room on a large armchair, which makes her look tiny.

The room is full of people, mostly wearing black. Some are drinking glasses of sherry or tea from china cups and saucers, others are eating food from a buffet laid out on a table at the back of the room. A woman from the catering company stands by the buffet to serve hot soup from a tureen.

There's another smaller table covered in flowers and cards, and there are other chairs pushed against walls – some of them straight-backed chairs which have been moved from the dining room.

ALICE's MUM, SUZANNE, sits in a corner on a dining room chair. A couple of guests are speaking to her, offering condolences.

ALICE's DAD, GRAHAM, hovers nearby.

In another corner ALICE's GRANDDAD, mostly asleep in a wheelchair, is being looked after by two elderly friends from the old folks' home.

ALICE's AUNT and UNCLE are separately talking to other clusters of guests.

Elsewhere, a middle-aged man, a TEACHER from ALICE's school, is talking to two diffident-looking boys of about seventeen, dressed as smartly as their mothers could persuade them, but with emo haircuts and very skinny trousers. We hear snippets of conversations from all around the room.

TEACHER: You don't often get a proper cup and saucer, do you?

GUEST: Lovely flowers.

AUNTIE: So young. Seventeen. What a waste.

GUEST: I mean it's not like you can say it was a mercy, is it?

GUEST: Lovely service.

AUNTIE: It's quite nice sherry, actually.

TEACHER: Difficult to know what to say, isn't it?

GUEST: We're very sorry for your loss.

GUEST: Seventeen!

TEACHER: What I remember most is how much he made you all laugh.

AUNTIE: I cannot *imagine* what it's like. To lose a child.

(To her son.) Stand up straight, Christopher, have some respect.

MUM: Thank you, thanks for coming. Have you had a drink?

AUNTIE sneezes.

AUNTIE: And you know, Alice *adored* him.

The guests move away from MUM. AUNTIE sneezes.

I'm so sorry, it's all these flowers.

GUEST: You see those flowers tied to railings, don't you, but you never think –

The TEACHER comes up to MUM and DAD. The teenage boys (TOM and DAN) watch him from across the room.

TEACHER: It was a nice service, I thought. Just the right tone.

DAD: Thank you. Thanks for reading.

GUEST: Terrible thing, drink driving.

TEACHER: Well poetry's very much my thing. Joe said he liked Larkin, so –

DAN: So weird seeing Hunter here.

TOM: Numpty Hunter. He's actually more scary when he's being nice.

DAN: I'm starving.

TOM: Have a sandwich.

DAN: Mum said don't eat anything, leave it for the proper guests.

AUNTIE comes up to ALICE and hands her a piece of quiche on a plate.

AUNTIE: Eat this, love, you've got to eat.

ALICE nods and puts the plate of quiche on her lap. She looks at it, then at her mum.

TEACHER: And the photo wall is lovely.

DAD: We wanted to – you know, to pay tribute, to um, to celebrate his life.

TEACHER: Important to remember the good times.

MUM: Crack open the champagne. Why not?

Across the room the CATERER drops a plate, which shatters.

ALICE's MUM jumps at the sound, looking across the room.

For god's sake!

DAD: Suzanne –

MUM: Well what's she doing? God's sake.

DAD: It's fine, just an accident.

A young male WAITER wearing a white shirt and long white butcher-style apron swoops in with a dustpan and brush to help the caterer clean up the mess.

AUNTIE comes up to MUM with another piece of quiche on a plate and hands it to her.

AUNTIE: You've not eaten, Suzie, you should eat something –

AUNTIE moves off again.

MUM: Nobody calls me Suzie anymore.

(To teacher, holding out her plate.) Would you like some quiche?

TEACHER: I can't actually eat eggs, so –

MUM: Well, there's soup.

TEACHER: Yes, I might have some soup.

The WAITER is passing. MUM hands her plate to him.

MUM: Sorry, can I give this to – sorry, I can't eat it.

ALICE, seeing this, puts her plate of quiche on the floor beside her armchair, untouched. She looks at her mum.

DAN: Sod it, I'm having a sandwich.

They start to head towards the buffet table, but are intercepted by ALICE's DAD.

DAD: Alright lads? Some pictures of you with Joe on the photo collage – Should have got you to play, shouldn't we? Bit of music.

DAN: Yeah, be a bit –

TOM: Bit weird.

GUEST: And of course Alice adored him.

GUEST: Lovely flowers.

GUEST: D'you know she's not left the house since it happened?

DAN: We're splitting the band up probably, so –

DAD: What, musical differences?

ALICE's COUSIN, a young man aged around 19 sits down next to her, too close for comfort.

COUSIN: Hi. All these people, huh? Who are they all, you know?

You know you can talk to me, don't you? If you ever need comforting or – We could go for a drink or whatever.

ALICE: I'm twelve.

COUSIN: No, I know, I know. I didn't –

You're twelve? Hands up – thought you were older.

ALICE: Piss off.

COUSIN: Language.

ALICE: English.

Her COUSIN gets up.

COUSIN: Sorry you lost your brother.

ALICE: I didn't *lose* him.

Her COUSIN moves away.

GUEST: Just doesn't seem fair, does it?

AUNTIE comes over to MUM, who is looking over at the buffet table. AUNTIE is carrying two glasses of sherry.

MUM: Gannets – look at them all.

AUNTIE: *(Handing her a sherry.)* Have a drink, love.

MUM: You're having another, are you? She's had four of those. Gannets.

AUNTIE: This is my first. D'you think there's enough sandwiches? Plenty of soup left, so – Good to give people something hot.

MUM: When did you last see us? When did you last see Joe?

AUNTIE: Last year, wasn't it?

MUM: Three years.

AUNTIE moves away from MUM towards ALICE. She sneezes.

AUNTIE: Oh dear, all these flowers.

GUEST: Lovely flowers.

GUEST: Lovely service.

GUEST: Lovely service.

GUEST: Lovely flowers.

There's a sudden burst of loud music – everyone dances to it, like a strange jerky version of the Twist. ALICE looks around in amazement.

After a few seconds the music and the dancing stops, and everyone goes back to what they were doing before.

ALICE's AUNTIE comes over to the big armchair.

AUNTIE: Alright, Alice? D'you want a cup of tea or anything?

ALICE: I'll have a whisky, please.

GUEST: Time's a great healer, you know.

UNCLE: How's the soup?

TEACHER: Bit peppery if I'm honest.

AUNTIE perches awkwardly on the arm of the chair.

AUNTIE: It's OK to have a cry, you know, let it all out. He was a darling boy, your brother.

AUNTIE looks as if she might cry. She looks for a tissue. ALICE hands her one.

You just have to give it time. Why don't you go outside with the other children?

ALICE stands up, moves towards her mum.

Bit of fresh air might make you feel better.

AUNTIE stands up, rubbing her back. She downs the rest of her sherry, then looks over to her husband.

David?

GUEST: I mean you never know what life's going to throw at you next.

UNCLE: *(Showing the teacher his watch.)* Water resistant to 600 feet, and that's a compass and it's got a stopwatch as well.

AUNTIE: David, I need you to rub my back, it's killing me.

UNCLE: Not here, love.

AUNTIE: I am in *constant* pain right now.

UNCLE rubs AUNTIE's back, and she makes contented noises.

Somewhere else in the room someone laughs, then stifles it.

ALICE hovers close to her MUM. DAD is standing by her now.

MUM: Not very appropriate.

DAD: Helen's being very helpful.

MUM: Sick of her fussing over me. Where's she been for three years, you know, where was she when mum was ill?

ALICE: Mum?

MUM: Not now, Alice. Do something useful.

AUNTIE : *(To Teacher.)* Alice didn't go to the service, you know.

GUEST: Of course Alice adored him.

AUNTIE: She's not been out the house since it happened. Two whole weeks shut in here.

A couple of little boys wearing heelies come through, scattering adults in their wake.

MUM: God's sake – those are not suitable shoes for – Whose children are they?

DAD goes after the two boys.

DAD: Now boys, where's your mum and dad?

MUM moves too, nearly bumping into ALICE.

MUM: Alice, will you get out from under my feet?

GUEST: It'll get better with time.

GUEST: Doesn't seem fair, does it?

GUEST: Take it one day at a / time.

GUEST: Time's a great healer.

TEACHER: We all miss you at school, you know. D'you think you might want to come back soon? See all your friends?

ALICE: Don't know yet.

TEACHER: You mustn't just think of me as mean old Mr Hunter, you know. Come and find me any time if you need a chat.

15

ALICE: Thanks.

GUEST: There's a *lot* of pepper in these sandwiches. Big lumps of it.

GUEST: But the flowers are lovely.

GUEST: The flowers are lovely.

GUEST: And you know, Alice *adored* him.

A little girl comes up to ALICE, and holds out a cuddly toy towards her. It's a big, floppy white rabbit. ALICE takes it from the little girl.

ALICE: Thank you.

The little girl goes back to her mother, shyly. ALICE holds the rabbit, stroking its ears. ALICE goes back to the armchair.

On the other side of the room, someone laughs. ALICE looks at her MUM, to check her reaction, but she's talking animatedly to another group of guests.

MUM: Yes, there'll be a trial, definitely. As big and public as possible. I've said we won't settle out of court, no way.

DAD: Well we haven't actually decided that.

MUM: We owe it to Joe to see justice done.

GUEST: Lock him up and throw away the key.

GUEST: Time's a great healer.

DAD: Suze – When do we want to show the thing, love?

AUNTIE sidles over to join the conversation.

MUM: I mean that man doesn't have a leg to stand on, he'd been drinking. And then he goes speeding around past a school at chucking-out time.

AUNTIE: Have to live with it his whole life.

MUM: Good. They should bring back the death penalty for people like him.

DAD: Suze –

MUM: String him up, cut his head off.

AUNTIE: Very civilised.

MUM: You know what, Helen, it's none of your business.

GUEST: You have to remember the good times.

AUNTIE: I don't know what I've done to make you so angry at me. I'm very sorry Joe's passed away, but –

MUM: He didn't *pass away*, he died in massive pain at the side of the road, so let's not. Let's not sugar it.

The WAITER comes up to ALICE, checks no-one is looking and surreptitiously hands her a small glass of white wine. ALICE glances at her mum, then takes the glass. She looks up at the WAITER to say thank you, but he moves away smoothly.

The two elderly friends of ALICE's granddad come over to MUM and DAD and AUNTIE. LEN is putting on a deerstalker hat, JIM a flat cap.

LEN: Er, Graham – Jim and I thought we'd take your dad off now. Hop on't bus back up Grenoside.

JIM: Very sorry for your loss, Mrs Little. At least he had a good innings.

MUM: He was seventeen.

DAD: Jim's on autopilot, that's all. Don't worry about it. Listen, don't go for a minute, I was just about to show everyone something.

DAD goes out towards the hall.

LEN: We're actually having a bit of trouble finding your dad's hat.

DAD: Oh, um. OK. In the hall?

MUM: It's over there on the buffet.

The hat is on the buffet table, on top of a plate of sausage rolls.

LEN: Alf, did you put your hat on't sausage rolls, silly bugger?

They go to retrieve GRANDDAD's hat.

GUEST: I thought the flowers were lovely.

GUEST: She's not been out the house, you know. Two weeks!

AUNTIE: I mean it's just SO sad. He was here and now he's gone.

UNCLE: Alright, love. You've had one too many sherries, that's all.

The WAITER wheels a large TV into the middle of the room, with ALICE's DAD following behind.

DAD: Hi everyone – hi –

Sorry, can I just have your –

The room goes quiet.

Thanks. Thanks.

So, Suzanne and I just wanted to say –

Thank you, for –

MUM leaves the room.

For being here today, it means a lot to us. And. We found this – this bit of video, which we don't think any of you will have seen because we think it was the last thing he ever recorded, so –

Sorry.

So we wanted to show it to you. If you'd all like to gather round.

The guests all gather round to watch the TV. ALICE is in the middle of the group.

DAD speaks to the WAITER, to get him to start the tape.

OK, thank you.

The guests watch as JOE's voice, and then ALICE's, come out of the screen.

JOE: *(Laughing.)* ...Come on, don't get the face on, I'm recording it now.

ALICE: *(On screen.)* I don't want to –

JOE: Right then, here it is, ladies and gentlemen, this is Alice's birthday song…

(Strums a chord, sings the Artic Monkeys.) Now then mardy bum…

In the video, ALICE comes over and hits him on the head. He laughs.

Ow.

The guests all look at ALICE.

ALICE: *(On screen.)* Stop doing stupid songs.

In the video, ALICE stamps out of the room.

JOE: Al – come back, I've got your – It took me ages, come on.

OK, Alice is in a mard, so here's her song and she can watch it when she's feeling better. Happy Birthday Bumface.

(sings)
This song is like your brother, slightly rubbish but it's yours,
Goes round and round inside your head,
It never seems to pause or finish.
But after quite a time you find it kind of wears you down,
Pretending not to listen but you're struggling to frown.
(It's your birthday.) So don't frown.

This song is like your brother, it'll try to make you laugh,
And when it learns to drive you'll find it
Drops you off, picks you up from places.
It helps you with your homework, it'll help you find your phone
It helps you feel less frightened and alone.
You're not alone.

So Happy Birthday Alice,
This little song's for you,
It's not very original,
Your brother's quite a throwback.

It's the only thing I've got you
It's the most I can afford
'Cause of spending all my money on a
Skateboard.

This song is like your brother, it prefers its pizza cold,
And also, like your brother it'll
Be here when you're old and weary.
This song is like your brother, this brother's like your song,
It's got your back it'll come back every
Birth – day – from – now – on…

Into riff on 'Happy Birthday etc…'

The other guests disappear, until ALICE is left alone, watching the TV, lit only by the light from the screen. She is totally absorbed by the video.

The only things left are ALICE, the armchair (on a strangely-shaped piece of carpet) and the TV.

The TV starts to disappear through the floor. ALICE gets up and goes towards it, willing it to stay.

After a moment, ALICE looks around her, finally realising the house has gone, that she's alone in a blank space, with no idea where she is.

A pair of long white ears appears through the seat of the armchair, followed shortly by a white motorbike helmet, (which the ears are growing out of), and underneath that, wearing the helmet, a man all dressed in white.

He sees ALICE.

WHITE RABBIT: Right. Excellent. Here you are. All ready?

The WHITE RABBIT climbs out of the chair.

ALICE: What?

WHITE RABBIT: Good, I should go. Got your helmet?

He looks down, realising he's got his jacket on back to front.

Oh look at me.

He clumsily takes it off and puts it back on the right way round during the next (without noticing that it's also inside-out).

ALICE: Helmet?

WHITE RABBIT: Didn't they tell you?

ALICE: What, who?

WHITE RABBIT: Have you got any kind of hard hat with you?

ALICE: A hat?

WHITE RABBIT: Have you ever played that game where everything you say has to be a question?

ALICE: Game?

WHITE RABBIT: Yup, yes, very good.

ALICE: I wasn't playing a –

That's still inside out.

WHITE RABBIT: Oh. Dear.

He takes his jacket off again and turns it outside-out before putting it back on.

So you haven't got a hard hat?

ALICE: No, um –

WHITE RABBIT: I'm sure you'll be fine, just look out for the cabbages. Pretty lethal if you don't see them coming.

Right, good, I must go.

The WHITE RABBIT goes back towards the armchair, in a hurry.

ALICE: Where you going?

WHITE RABBIT: I've got to, um –

ALICE: You can't go, what am I supposed to –

WHITE RABBIT: You want me to stay here?

ALICE: I mean – I mean – what's going on? What is this?

WHITE RABBIT: Right right yeah yeah.

Yeah, I'm not really *supposed* to –

It'll get explained to you once you're inside.

ALICE: Once I'm inside what? I don't want to go inside anything.

WHITE RABBIT: I think actually, it's not really, um. Optional.

ALICE: What?

WHITE RABBIT: Don't shoot the messenger, OK? It's pretty – Difficult to explain.

ALICE: Sorry. Sorry.

Where's my family? Where's all our things?

WHITE RABBIT: Where they always were. Mostly.

ALICE: Are you being deliberately –

WHITE RABBIT: There's things I can't tell you yet.

ALICE: Why?

WHITE RABBIT: Because you've sort of got to work them out for yourself?

ALICE: OK. Well. I prefer having the answer and then working back from it, I'm that sort of –

The WHITE RABBIT looks at his watch, trying to be surreptitious, but ALICE sees.

Sorry, am I keeping you?

WHITE RABBIT: What?

ALICE: Tell me what's going on.

WHITE RABBIT: OK.

OK. You've gone into a kind of hole. A kind of –

It's called a rabbit hole. Hence the, um *(He points to his ears.)*

ALICE: What am I here for?

WHITE RABBIT: There's something you need to go through
before you can go back.

ALICE: What if I don't want to 'go through' something?

WHITE RABBIT: You don't really have a choice. The longer
you fight it, the longer you'll stay, actually. I'm told.

ALICE: Stay here. In this room?

WHITE RABBIT: Yup.

ALICE: With you?

WHITE RABBIT: Not so much.

ALICE: But I can't just –

You know, my parents are going to be really cross if I've
gone off somewhere, they'll be really cross at you.

WHITE RABBIT: I think they've got other things on their
minds, haven't they?

ALICE turns away from him. The WHITE RABBIT looks at his watch.

ALICE: *(In a small voice.)* So what do I have to do?

WHITE RABBIT: Good question. Um.

He tries to remember.

Hang on – I wrote it down somewhere.

*He starts to go through his pockets. He pulls out various scraps of
paper.*

Something about 'you've got to' – oh what was it?

He looks at a piece of paper.

Here we go – no that's a receipt for some beans –

Oh, what was it? I did say it shouldn't be my job to –

ALICE: I really quite need to know.

WHITE RABBIT: Yeah I know I know. Something about a *heart*
– like, um, anyone who had a *heart*, or – total eclipse of the
heart, or –

ALICE: Heart attack?

WHITE RABBIT: That's it! 'You've got to go right to the heart'.

ALICE: What does that mean?

WHITE RABBIT: You know, I'd love to stay here chatting but I've really got to get. On.

The WHITE RABBIT goes to the armchair and picks up one corner of the carpet underneath it – it turns out to be rigid, and he folds it upwards. He continues to do so with the other corners, eventually making a wooden box (the same colour as the floor) which encloses the armchair.

ALICE: But what does 'go right to the Heart' mean?

WHITE RABBIT: You'll work it out. Think of it like a lovely crossword or treasure hunt or something –

ALICE: What you doing?

WHITE RABBIT: You'll be alright, you'll find everything you need, don't worry.

ALICE: You said I needed a hard hat –

WHITE RABBIT: DUCK!

ALICE ducks, frightened. Nothing else happens. After a second she straightens up again.

Good reflexes, you'll be fine.

The WHITE RABBIT climbs into the box, now fully constructed.

Go right to the heart – all you need to do.

The WHITE RABBIT closes the lid, shutting himself inside the box. ALICE runs towards it.

ALICE: No, wait, where are you –

ALICE tries to find the lid of the box.

How does this open? How does this –

ALICE hammers on the box with her fist.

Come out I want to talk to you.

Please come out.

Please don't leave me.

The box starts to sink into/through the floor.

No no no no no no no.

Wait, don't –

Don't go. Please.

ALICE kicks the box, angry.

Don't bloody leave me here.

She kicks the box again, hurting her foot this time. She sinks to the floor, clutching her foot.

Ow that hurt that hurt.

ALICE watches the box disappear through the floor, and the floor seal itself up again.

She looks up. She looks around at an almost bare room.

So what's –

Where. Is –

Who. Was –

Who. Um. Am –

She stands up. Her foot still hurts from kicking the box.

Where's my mum and dad?

Ow. Ow, that. Ow. Ow that hurts.

Where's the man gone with the ear things, rabbit things, ears?

Not here.

Ow.

OK. Get out. If you can get in, got to be able to get out, surely.

I mean, how did I – How did I get in?

Where's the door?

Where would they put the door?

If I was making this room, where would I put the door?

Ow, is that a splinter?

If I was a complete mentalist and I was making a deliberately confusing room, where would I put the door?

On the ceiling.

ALICE looks up.

There isn't a ceiling. Brilliant.

ALICE looks down again and sees a table over the other side of the room.

That – That wasn't there. That was not there – that's come from –

Where did that come from?

It must've – I must just not've seen it it's OK.

ALICE goes over to the table. There's a key on it. ALICE picks it up.

OK. OK, for what?

ALICE turns around. There's a tiny door across the other side of the room.

Right. Is that –

If that's the way out then it's a rubbish one, if that's the only way out.

Is that seriously the –

How'm I supposed to get through that?

This is stupid.

ALICE looks at the table. There's a small bottle on it which wasn't there before.

Um, no. No – who put that there?

She looks around.

Seriously, who put that there?

I don't think this is funny, by the way. I think this is just. Actually *childish*, so –

ALICE goes over to the table and looks at the bottle.

And this is and this is and this is what is this?

'Drink Me'

Drink Me. Good idea bad idea? Bad idea. Don't be a dick.

Alice puts the bottle down on the table and steps away from it.

What would Joe do?

Step of the kerb without looking. Of course.

ALICE goes over to the little bottle and drinks about half of it.

Quite nice, actually. Popcorn? Is it popcorn? Buttered toast.

She looks at the door again. It's now the size of a normal door.

Big door.

That *grew* when I –

Or did I *shrink*? Did I shrink?

God this is –

Maybe I shrank. Maybe I'm tiny. Have I shrunk?

Whatever – result! Good result! Going through the door –

ALICE goes to the door and tries the handle, but it won't open.

What? Come on.

She turns around to look at where the table was, but because she's shrunk, it now towers over her.

No no no no no

The key the key the key where's the key where's the key

Where's the key

Where's the key

Where's the bloody key?

She looks up, realises it's still on the top of the table.

Oh god.

ALICE makes an attempt to climb the leg of the table, but there's nothing to hold on to, it's too slippery.

I can't do it without the key.

Her attention is caught by a small cake on the floor.

I said *key* not *cake*.

She looks at the cake.

'Eat Me'

That looks nice, actually. Yeah, Stranger Danger. Don't eat the sweets.

What happens if I eat it?

What happens if I don't?

She bites into the cake very carefully, then after a moment in which nothing terrible happens, she takes another bite, and another.

That's actually really nice.

Three bites into it she puts a hand to her stomach.

Ooh, Alton Towers…

It seems to go away, so she carries on eating the cake.

This is so much nicer than Mr Kiplings. What's in that icing?

ALICE is distracted by the cake and doesn't notice that she's growing – the table shrinks back to normal size and the door is replaced by a tiny one.

When she finishes the cake, ALICE looks at the table.

Oh yay, have I grown? I've grown.

ALICE runs over to the table.

The key the key the key.

She picks up the key.

The key!

She's about to turn around when she stops dead.

Oh no.

She turns round to have her suspicion proved true – the door has also shrunk.

Oh no.

It's like a computer game, this. I hate computer games.

This is bloody stupid.

She's about to give up, when she looks down and sees the bottle in her hand.

OK.

Computer game.

She drinks part of the liquid left in the bottle, then turns back and looks at the door. It's now medium-sized.

Good good good

She drinks the rest of the bottle down, facing away from the door, and when she turns back, it's normal-sized.

OK. Here we go. Got the key, got the door, here we go.

She goes over to the door and puts the key in the lock.

With a great clanking sound the entire back wall concertinas open to reveal what seems to be a massive cupboard, a huge jumble of mad things and madder people.

ALICE peers into the gloom behind the door. Various figures are dimly visible but strange and unnerving.

A small mechanical toy wheels out of the gloom and whizzes past ALICE, along the floor. She follows it, her attention drawn away from the world behind the door.

As ALICE is looking the other way, a voice calls out from the gloom, amplified by a megaphone.

CATERPILLAR: Stay where you are.

ALICE looks around, unsure where the voice is coming from. She moves a step or two.

I *said.* Stay where you are.

ALICE: Is someone there?

Out of the gloom, a low vehicle comes towards ALICE, much like a chaise longue, but with many wheels. A large CATERPILLAR is reclined on it, speaking from a megaphone.

He's followed by a team of minions – these are Wonderlanders, citizens of the state of Wonderland.

The chaise longue stops at a short distance from ALICE. The CATERPILLAR pauses and blows into what looks like a hookah attached to the chaise longue – when he blows into it, bubbles come out.

CATERPILLAR: Trying to sneak across the border, were you?

ALICE: What border?

CATERPILLAR: By the power invested in me by the King and Queen of Wonderland I command you to cooperate with state immigration policy.

ALICE: I can hear you fine you don't need the thing.

CATERPILLAR: Stand behind the line until you're invited to approach the desk.

ALICE: What line? What desk?

The WONDERLANDERS use some tape to create a line in front of ALICE. Then they erect a desk across the caterpillar's lap. They hand him various pieces of paper, which he scrutinises, and either eats or rubber stamps.

Sorry, what do I –

CATERPILLAR: Wait until you're called forward. You're not the only person here, you know.

ALICE looks behind her.

ALICE: I sort of am.

The WONDERLANDERS watch her carefully, pretending that they aren't.

She takes out her mobile phone and looks at it. No signal.

She holds it above her head and all around her, looking for a signal.

(A swear word.) Arsene Wenger.

One of the WONDERLANDERS sees this and whispers to the CATERPILLAR. He looks at ALICE.

CATERPILLAR: Hand over the device.

ALICE: It's not a device it's just a – It's Pay As You Go.

CATERPILLAR: Are you failing to cooperate? Any failure to cooperate will result in immediate expulsion.

ALICE hands the phone to one of the WONDERLANDERS. He proceeds to take it apart on the desk. He takes the battery out of the back and sniffs it, then eats it, nodding appreciatively.

ALICE: That's mine, you can't – Don't eat it, it's not –

The other WONDERLANDERS crowd around with interest and proceed to eat the other parts of the phone.

The CATERPILLAR looks up from his paperwork.

CATERPILLAR: Step forward please.

ALICE: They've just eaten my phone.

CATERPILLAR: Just a few questions.

ALICE: They've *eaten* my phone.

CATERPILLAR: What's the purpose of your visit – business or pleasure?

ALICE: Um. Neither.

CATERPILLAR: I don't have to let you in, you know. If your answers are not satisfactory to me you'll stay right here until they are.

ALICE: Right. OK, sorry.

CATERPILLAR: Purpose of your visit?

ALICE: I really don't know. I mean I'm not trying to like, move here.

CATERPILLAR: How long do you plan to stay?

ALICE: Um. I don't know. The rabbit didn't say, so –

He said I have to go to the Heart, do you know where that is?

CATERPILLAR: We are the Wonderland State Border Control, not a tourist information office.

Take this form.

The CATERPILLAR hands a piece of paper to ALICE.

ALICE: Thank you. I haven't got a pen.

CATERPILLAR: You're supposed to fold it up nicely and give it back to me.

ALICE: Um. OK.

ALICE starts to fold up the paper.

CATERPILLAR: As interestingly as possible.

ALICE: OK, um. Like a paper aeroplane or –

CATERPILLAR: A swan, maybe?

ALICE: I can do an aeroplane.

CATERPILLAR: Fine.

ALICE makes a paper aeroplane during the next.

Are you now or have you ever been involved in terrorist activity?

ALICE: No.

CATERPILLAR: International espionage? Arms trading?

ALICE: Not as far as I know. No.

CATERPILLAR: Have you any pastry with you?

ALICE: Pastry?

CATERPILLAR: No filo, no puff, no pâté sucree?

ALICE: No.

CATERPILLAR: No jams, marmalades, chutneys or other conserves or condiments about your person?

ALICE: What? No.

CATERPILLAR: You sure?

ALICE: Yes.

CATERPILLAR: Any baggage with you?

ALICE: No.

CATERPILLAR: Any emotional baggage?

ALICE: What?

CATERPILLAR: The State of Wonderland is an Emotional State. Do you have any emotional baggage?

ALICE: Um. No.

CATERPILLAR: That means yes. Could anyone have tampered with your emotional baggage without your knowledge?

ALICE: If they had, I wouldn't know, would I?

CATERPILLAR: PROCESS HER!

ALICE: What?

Some of the WONDERLANDERS surround ALICE. Others whip out instruments and start to play a song (this is the WONDERBAND). The WONDERLANDERS sing as they work.

CATERPILLAR: Arms out.

33

ALICE puts her arms out to the sides. One of the WONDERLANDERS pats her down.

WONDERLANDERS: *(Singing)*
When you're talking to the caterpillar
Don't be rude, remove your haterpillar
Don't you know he's where it's aterpillar
Better comply

CATERPILLAR: Open wide!

ALICE opens her mouth and one of the WONDERLANDERS takes a scrape from inside her cheek.

WONDERLANDERS: *(Singing)*
If he asks you what's the matterpillar
Can't rely on idle patterpillar
Or flirtatious gracious chatterpillar
Better not lie

During this verse one of the WONDERLANDERS pulls a hair out of ALICE's head.

ALICE: Ouch!

The hair is transferred to an envelope with tweezers, in the manner of a forensic expert on CSI.

The WONDERLANDERS break into the chorus of the song, a disconcertingly carnival tune:

WONDERLANDERS: *(Singing)*
Welcome to Wonderland!
Enjoy the Wonderband!
There's nothing underhand about us!
Welcome to Wonderland!
If you've got contraband
This is the time for you to give it up

CATERPILLAR: Body scan!

One of the WONDERLANDERS uses an old bedpan on a long stick to scan ALICE's body (like a long-handled metal detector). He makes a beeping noise with his mouth when the scanner is close to Alice's pockets.

WONDERLANDERS: *(Singing softly as dialogue between ALICE and CATERPILLAR continues)*
When you're talking to the caterpillar
Don't be rude, remove your haterpillar
Don't you know he's where it's aterpillar
Better comply

If he asks you what's the matterpillar
Can't rely on idle patterpillar
Or flirtatious gracious chatterpillar
Better not lie

CATERPILLAR: Empty your pockets.

ALICE empties her pockets – a lip balm and a couple of sweets – onto the CATERPILLAR's desk.

The WONDERLANDER scans her again. The scanner beeps again near her pocket.

ALICE: He's making that noise with his mouth.

CATERPILLAR: What else have you got in there?

ALICE: It's nothing, it –

CATERPILLAR: Take it out!

ALICE pulls a plectrum out of her pocket.

ALICE: Look – It's just – it's just a plectrum.

CATERPILLAR: Give it to me.

ALICE: I can't, it's very important.

CATERPILLAR: Put it on the desk.

The WONDERLANDERS' singing peters out as they get distracted by listening…

ALICE: You mustn't eat it.

ALICE puts the plectrum on the CATERPILLAR's desk.

It's my brother's. Was my brother's.

He picks up the plectrum.

CATERPILLAR: A what?

ALICE: Plectrum. It's for playing guitar.

CATERPILLAR: Plec. Trum.

Looks to me very much like a fluting device. Looks very much like the sort of tool you'd use to crimp the edges of some kind of confection, something made out of pastry, perhaps a *tart.*

ALICE: It's for music. Please –

The CATERPILLAR clicks his fingers, and the WONDERLANDERS very carefully put the plectrum into an envelope, like they did with the hair sample.

Please, it's the only thing I've –

CATERPILLAR: You can have it back when you leave.

The CATERPILLAR picks up a rubber stamp.

How long did you say you intend to stay?

ALICE: I didn't. I don't know.

CATERPILLAR: Let's just take it one day at a time, then shall we? I'm issuing you with a one-day visa. If you need to stay longer you'll have to come back tomorrow.

WONDERLANDER: Beep beep beep! Illegal immigrant in sector 27!

CATERPILLAR: Onward!

The WONDERLANDERS start to wheel the CATERPILLAR away.

ALICE: Hang on –

CATERPILLAR: Quickly now!

ALICE: But what do I – what do I do now?

CATERPILLAR: We are the Wonderland State Border Control, not a haberdashery.

ALICE: But where's the border? If you're the border control.

CATERPILLAR: You've crossed it.

The WONDERLANDERS wheel the caterpillar off, humming the Welcome To Wonderland tune.

ALICE turns around, looking behind her, but there's no obvious border there.

ALICE: This place is mental.

ALICE is surrounded by other WONDERLANDERS carrying enormous flowers above their heads. Almost as soon as they're there, they're gone.

Then a procession of WONDERLANDERS carrying open umbrellas, followed by a man taking a cabbage for a walk. He stops, as if the cabbage is a dog having a poo. Then leans down with a plastic bag over his hand, and picks up a sprout, which he bags and bins.

A POSTMAN arrives, pulling a post box on wheels.

POSTMAN: Aha, yes, you – you're off to see the Duchess.

ALICE: Am I?

POSTMAN: In about 90 seconds time.

ALICE: *(To herself.)* OK, right, yeah. Computer game.

POSTMAN: In which case you can take something in for me, hang on a jiffy bag…

The POSTMAN opens the door of the letter box and starts to search through it, pulling out lots of things that aren't letters – a cuddly toy, saucepan, bunch of flowers, a basketball, a fireguard, some bellows, a string of bunting…

ALICE watches him.

ALICE: Has she got a dog or something?

POSTMAN: No no. Sure it's here somewhere…

ALICE: Why don't you want to go in there?

POSTMAN: I'd be perfectly happy to go in there.

ALICE: OK, just thought you were –

POSTMAN: I'M NOT SCARED OF HER.

ALICE: OK.

POSTMAN: Bells and whistles, where's this letter? Ooh, here we are.

The POSTMAN pulls a letter out of the postbox.

He hands the letter to ALICE.

Thought I'd lost another one, there. Lose my head if I'm not careful.

Got one for you, too.

He hands ALICE another letter.

ALICE turns the letter over in her hand. The POSTMAN starts to leave.

Cheerio then.

He stops.

Oh, and if the Duchess offers you a bowl of soup, best say you've already had your tea.

ALICE: But I don't know where her house is.

POSTMAN: You're there already.

ALICE looks around and finds herself in a hot, steamy kitchen. She puts both letters in her pocket.

The room is filled with steam and the smell of drains. On a table are piles of festering vegetables and rotting fish, and a couple of tea towels so dirty they're stuck to the surface and growing whole new species of bacteria in their folds.

A large saucepan bubbles on a stove, giving off filthy looking fumes.

ALICE: Oh my god. Yuck.

What is that? Euw, yuck yuck yuck.

ALICE sneezes.

'Choo!

OK, if it's computer game – where do I click?

'Choo!

What am I supposed to pick up?

I don't want to pick anything up it all looks disgusting.

ALICE sees the COOK bustling about (he'd been indistinguishable from a big pile of dirty rags at the start.).

Oh. Sorry. 'Choo!

Sorry, I was just talking to – Um.

'Choo! Sorry it's a bit, um, something's making me –

The COOK doesn't look at ALICE, but continues bustling, wielding a scary-looking meat cleaver as he hacks up a teddy bear and puts the pieces in a roasting tin.

ALICE looks around. All of a sudden, the WHITE RABBIT dashes in, in a mad rush, as if pursued.

Hey – hello – hi – 'Choo!

The WHITE RABBIT jumps into the pot of soup on the stove.

Hey, wait, hang on –

ALICE runs over to the soup pot and climbs up onto the work surface to look inside it, but the rabbit isn't in there.

ALICE lifts the ladle to find it contains only soup.

How did you – How did he do that?

ALICE stirs the pot, but to no avail. She turns to the COOK.

Sorry, did you just see the White Rabbit jump in here?

COOK doesn't seem to hear her. He coats the teddy bear pieces in olive oil, tosses and places the whole thing in the oven (or in the soup pot).

The cook grabs an enormous pepper grinder and grinds it into the soup.

Oh my gosh – 'Choo! – is that supposed to have so much –

'Choo! – Is it that what's making me sneeze?

Sorry, can't you talk?

The COOK opens his mouth to speak, but before he can get a word out, the DUCHESS sweeps in.

DUCHESS: Cookie! A visitor! How lovely!

She's dressed in her idea of a perfect 1950s housewife, except her clothes are filthy and stained and her hair is wild. She's holding a baby, tightly bundled in a blanket, who cries incessantly.

Baby, we've got a visitor!

The baby responds with a loud fart, a small sneeze and more wailing.

Ahh, he likes you already, see.

How nice of you to come and see us. Cookie, you should have told me we had a guest.

ALICE: Yeah, I'm actually –

DUCHESS: Don't mind baby, he's just expressing himself, aren't you baby?

Aren't you a beautiful baby baby baby PIG baby baby.

The baby farts again. The DUCHESS grimaces, then covers it.

ALICE: I wanted to speak to the White Rabbit only he went in that saucepan, so –

DUCHESS: In the soup? Cookie, did you put a rabbit in the soup? You know, food is my *passion* – I hope it was organic, Cookie, and fair trade and locally produced and seasonal –

ALICE: Thing is, it's not a rabbit-sized rabbit, more a man-sized rabbit. I mean, it's not an eating rabbit, it's a –

DUCHESS: Baby's a very adventurous eater, aren't you, baby, he'll eat anything, broccoli, pine cones, compost…

ALICE: 'Cause I really need to talk to him you see – 'Choo!

DUCHESS: I mean the number of things I've pureed for baby and he'll just snaffle it up like a little –

ALICE: 'Choo!

DUCHESS: People say how d'you find the time, all that
pureeing I say I don't know it just comes naturally like on
some level I feel I've always been a mother, I'm just a very
nurturing person –

Have a muffin – I made them.

*The DUCHESS thrusts a plate of muffins at ALICE. They're covered
in cobwebs and appear to have fish heads sticking out of the top.*

ALICE: Are those fish?

DUCHESS: I'm into slow food, aren't you? Go on, have a
lovely warm muffin.

ALICE: No thanks, I really need to –

DUCHESS: You don't need to worry about your weight, you're
tiny!

ALICE: I'm not worried about my *weight* I'm just –

DUCHESS: Or some soup? We always have a pot of soup on
the go for when visitors come, only no-one ever does, do
they Cookie?

ALICE: Yeah, I really need to find the rabbit because he gave
me this, um, mission sort of thing –

DUCHESS: Why don't you tell me about it, eh? Sit and have a
girly natter – why don't I brush your hair for you?

*The DUCHESS pulls out a revolting brush, matted with hair and
other horrors. ALICE backs off.*

ALICE: No no, I don't – Um, cause I've only got a one day
visa, you see, and I'd really rather not –

DUCHESS: And then we can go shopping together.

ALICE: OK, maybe you know where I'm supposed to go – I'm
looking for something called the Heart.

DUCHESS: I know! Let's give each other a facial!

ALICE: Do you know where that is, the Heart?

DUCHESS: Of course I know where it is.

ALICE: Yes? Where?

DUCHESS: *Home* is where the heart is, isn't it?

ALICE: Yeah, well I'm trying to get –

DUCHESS: And you're home now, so –

Why don't you stay forever, you could move in, we'll be like flatmates, we can borrow each others' clothes and run each other baths and things –

The queen used to love it when I ran her a bath. We were like sisters really, only she got in a tizz about some silly –

ALICE: The queen?

DUCHESS: You know what it's like – having a baby can really get in the way of your –

The baby farts then sneezes.

SHUT UP!

I mean shush shush baby baby lovely baby.

Queenie thinks she doesn't like babies or something, silly billy, who doesn't like babies – she doesn't invite me to anything anymore, silly billy.

Now baby, how about a bit of hush for mummy?

The DUCHESS bounces the baby in a way which looks rather rough.

Bouncy bouncy boo! And a bouncy bouncy boo! And a bouncy bouncy boo!

ALICE: Careful, he'll –

DUCHESS: Would you like to hold him?

ALICE: Um. No, look, I really ought to go.

DUCHESS: Don't go, don't be silly, you haven't had your tea yet.

ALICE: Yeah, had my tea before I came I'm sorry I've really got to –

ALICE starts to move away.

DUCHESS: No don't go don't go don't go don't go

DON'T LEAVE ME HERE WITH THE BABY!

I mean. I mean. You're my best friend.

ALICE: We've only just met.

DUCHESS: You don't know what it's like. No one comes. Even the postman won't stop and talk anymore, everyone's so *busy* –

ALICE: Oh, the postman –

DUCHESS: But now I've got you, haven't I? Now there'll always be someone there for me, all day every day, I can't tell you how happy we'll be all together – we don't ever need to go anywhere, we can just stay here with the curtains closed and be very very happy all by ourselves. Forever.

The baby farts.

PIG!

ALICE takes the DUCHESS's letter out of her pocket.

ALICE: Sorry, are you – Are you a Duchess?

DUCHESS: Of course I'm a Duchess. Don't I look like a Duchess?

ALICE: The postman gave me this for you.

DUCHESS: A letter? A letter? Open it!

ALICE: OK, um.

ALICE opens the letter.

DUCHESS: What can it be, baby? A letter for us!

ALICE: Um, it's an invitation. 'Choo!

The DUCHESS squeals with delight.

DUCHESS: An invitation! Did you hear that, Cookie? Who's it from who's it from?

ALICE: Um, the queen.

The DUCHESS screams like an excited teenage girl, making the baby scream even louder.

DUCHESS: The queen! She wants me back! This is it, Cookie – I knew she'd miss me, I knew she couldn't be without me for long!

ALICE: She wants you to come to a croquet match followed by tea and tarts –

The DUCHESS screams.

DUCHESS: Tea! Tarts! Dress Code?

ALICE: Dress Code: No babies.

DUCHESS: Ah. Right. No babies.

No no, well. I can see why you wouldn't want any babies at a croquet match –

Cookie, d'you think you could –

The DUCHESS looks over to the table, to see the COOK hacking up another cuddly toy. COOK looks up from the work and glares at the DUCHESS.

No, nothing dear.

The DUCHESS looks at ALICE.

Party game!

ALICE: Sorry?

DUCHESS: To celebrate.

ALICE: I've still got to go, though, so –

DUCHESS: Cookie – bring the plates.

ALICE: The game has plates?

DUCHESS: Spread out everyone.

The COOK and the DUCHESS form two points of a triangle, with ALICE being the other point.

Now, this is what you have to do –

ALICE sees that the COOK has turned towards the DUCHESS, and is swinging a plate, ready to throw it.

ALICE: No!

DUCHESS: Catch!

The DUCHESS throws the baby to ALICE, who catches it safely. The DUCHESS catches the plate.

There, you see.

The baby wriggles in ALICE's arms. She's quite shaken by the moment.

ALICE: Yeah, OK, I –

DUCHESS: Thank you, Cookie.

The DUCHESS starts to swing the plate to throw to ALICE.

ALICE: I don't think we need to do it ag –

The DUCHESS throws the plate.

Help!

ALICE throws the baby to the COOK, who catches it, having just thrown another plate to the DUCHESS.

They continue throwing the plates and the baby around in the circle.

What happens now?

DUCHESS: You keep going until the music stops.

ALICE: What music?

The WONDERBAND appear out of nowhere and play music.

The game continues, with the COOK and DUCHESS stepping back each time to widen the circle and make the throwing harder, to ALICE's dismay.

When the music stops, ALICE finds she's the one holding the baby.

DUCHESS: And that's the end of the game. Well done everyone, very good.

The baby farts.

Well done baby.

ALICE: Great – thank you, that was enormous –

ALICE tries to hand the baby back to the DUCHESS.

DUCHESS: No no, you must give the prizes.

ALICE: OK. Did someone win?

DUCHESS: Everybody won, and all must have prizes.

The COOK applauds, excited.

ALICE: Um, I haven't got – I haven't got anything.

DUCHESS: What have you got in your pocket?

ALICE goes for her pocket, struggling to keep hold of the baby, who's still wriggling. She pulls out a couple of small objects.

ALICE: I've got a lip balm and a lemon Starburst.

DUCHESS: Oh super!

The DUCHESS dashes in and grabs the lemon Starburst for herself. ALICE holds the lipbalm towards the COOK who snatches it. The DUCHESS stuffs the sweet into her mouth.

ALICE: Um, you have to take the paper off –

The COOK winds up the lip balm and takes a bite out of it. The DUCHESS starts to back away from ALICE.

DUCHESS: And your prize is the baby.

ALICE: Sorry, what?

DUCHESS: You get to keep the baby.

ALICE: No no, wait – No, hang on, you can't –

The COOK takes another bite of the lip balm and then also starts to back away.

DUCHESS: *(Departing.)* You're terribly good with him – he loves you.

ALICE: What am I going to do with a baby? Hello?

The baby wriggles.

Stop wriggling – like holding a jellyfish.

ALICE tries to follow the COOK and DUCHESS, but she can't hold the baby and move. As ALICE stands there, even the kitchen starts to retreat away from her.

Oh what, you're leaving as well, are you?

The kitchen stops momentarily, as if chastened, then continues to creep back away from her.

ALICE looks down at the baby in her arms. He's still screaming.

Oh please stop that.

ALICE tries bouncing the baby.

Come on – bouncy bouncy –

BABY: Oink!

ALICE: Pardon?

BABY: Oink!

ALICE looks at the BABY's face properly for the first time.

ALICE: Oh my god. You look like –

BABY: Oink!

The BABY wriggles free of its blankets and the head of a piglet appears, wearing a baby's bonnet.

ALICE: You're *actually* a pig. Oh god this is too weird.

The piglet wriggles so hard that ALICE is forced to let him down onto the floor.

OK, OK, you want to go –

The piglet dashes off on a winding course until out of sight.

No, wait – wait – you're not supposed to –

You're on your own, kid. Computer game's broken. I think I'm lost.

During this, a number of candy-striped poles grow up out of the floor. While they're still short, a couple of WONDERLANDERS, unseen by ALICE, attach arrow-shaped boards to the top of them so that they become signposts.

No, come on, Al, think properly. Got to find this Heart thing. OK, so it's not like *biologically* a heart because – I mean how could you *go* there, so –

So what else does heart mean?

The Heart means the middle, right, the middle of something? The centre.

So if I'm in a *place*, I've got to find the middle of it.

Except I haven't got a chuffing map.

ALICE looks around and sees the signposts.

Oh. OK. This is better.

ALICE goes to the signpost closer to her and tries to read the writing at the top of it. It says 'HERE', and points downwards.

Here. Ok, I'm here.

Behind ALICE a creature slinks across the stage in a rakish fashion – a self-styled lady killer in cowboy boots and a shirt with frilly cuffs. When he sees ALICE, he stops, his face breaking into a broad grin.

He stands still with a hand on his hip. The CHESHIRE CAT.

CHESHIRE CAT: Hello you.

ALICE looks at him.

I said, hello *you.*

ALICE: Hi.

ALICE goes back to looking at the other signposts.

CHESHIRE CAT: What's a gorgeous creature like you doing all alone?

ALICE: I'm not alone –

CHESHIRE CAT: That's a fib, naughty. Come over here, don't be unkind.

ALICE: I'm alright, thanks.

ALICE looks at another signpost. The CHESHIRE CAT sidles up to her without her realising.

And this one says 'There', which is there – so there's a place called here and a place called there –

CHESHIRE CAT: Mind if I rub against your leg?

ALICE jumps a little, looks at him with her best hard stare. He leans against one of the signposts, using it like a scratching pole. He smiles. It's unnerving.

ALICE: Why are you smiling?

CHESHIRE CAT: Why aren't you? It takes a lot more muscles to frown than smile, you know.

ALICE: Yeah, I need the exercise.

CHESHIRE CAT: Feisty – I like it.

The CAT starts to purr.

ALICE: What are you doing?

CHESHIRE CAT: It means I like you.

The CAT stretches his arms up.

Stroke my tummy.

ALICE: Do you know how old I am?

CHESHIRE CAT: Cat years?

ALICE: What?

Oh, OK, you're a cat.

CHESHIRE CAT: Stroke my tummy.

ALICE: I won't, if you don't mind.

God's sake, cats, rabbits…

The cat's ears prick up, he's suddenly alert.

CHESHIRE CAT: Rabbit? Where?

ALICE: No, not – Oh look please go away, I've got something I've got to do.

She looks at another sign.

This one says 'everywhere'. But it only points to one place.

The CAT plays with a swingball toy attached to the pole and it spins around.

Right, OK.

This doesn't make sense.

The CAT stops and looks at ALICE, arching his back and purring.

ALICE: Oh for god's –

CHESHIRE CAT: What?

ALICE: I wish you'd stop.

CHESHIRE CAT: Stop what?

ALICE: Trying to. Flirt me, or whatever.

CHESHIRE CAT: But you're lovely.

ALICE: Thanks, but. I'm busy.

CHESHIRE CAT: Fair dos, my darling. Thought you might need my help, that's all.

ALICE: Well I don't.

CHESHIRE CAT: Fine. Cheery-bye.

ALICE moves off, trying to look purposeful. The CAT sets to work attaching extra signs to the signposts. ALICE watches, surprised. The CAT continues to watch her out of the corner of his eye.

ALICE: OK, I do need some help. But I'm only asking 'cause you're the only person here.

CHESHIRE CAT: Flattery will get you everywhere.

ALICE: Just, since you've got signposts, you might be able to help me find the Heart.

CHESHIRE CAT: Ah, the Heart.

ALICE: Geographically.

CHESHIRE CAT: Yes yes.

ALICE: So?

CHESHIRE CAT: Stroke my tummy?

ALICE: No.

CHESHIRE CAT: Stroke my tummy. D'you want my help or not?

ALICE looks at him, realises he won't help unless she obliges. She reaches out and at arms' length scratches his tummy lightly with her fingertips.

He purrs.

ALICE: OK, that's enough. Which way do I go?

CHESHIRE CAT: Any way, really.

ALICE: Answer properly.

CHESHIRE CAT: Well read the signs.

The CAT shows her one of his signs. It reads 'H R TEA'

Look. Heart.

ALICE: But that doesn't say Heart.

CHESHIRE CAT: Yes it does.

ALICE: It says H.R. TEA.

CHESHIRE CAT: Spells Heart.

ALICE: But it doesn't.

CHESHIRE CAT: It does if you want it to.

ALICE: Where do I get to if I follow it?

CHESHIRE CAT: Exactly as it says – tea with the Hatter.

ALICE: It's short for Hatter Tea.

CHESHIRE CAT: Yes, my darling.

ALICE: OK, that doesn't really help. What about this one over here –

She goes to another sign. It also says H R TEA.

That says the same thing.

CHESHIRE CAT: No it doesn't.

ALICE: What?

CHESHIRE CAT: It says Hare Tea. That one's tea with the Hatter, this one's for tea with the Hare.

ALICE: Hare? Like a rabbit?

CHESHIRE CAT: Rabbit? Where?

ALICE: No, I mean –

So 'Hr' means Hatter and it means Hare as well?

CHESHIRE CAT: Yes.

ALICE: Great, so that's not confusing at all. And it doesn't help me decide which way to go, either. Hatter or Hare.

CHESHIRE CAT: They're both mad, of course.

ALICE: OK, can I go somewhere where there aren't any mad people?

CHESHIRE CAT: We're all mad here, sweetness.

ALICE: I'm not.

CHESHIRE CAT: You mustn't worry about a little thing like being mad.

ALICE: I'm not worried. I'm not mad.

CHESHIRE CAT: We're all mad here, we're all crazy as milkshake. Mad as a bag of trifle. You can't get past Border Control, you know, without demonstrating certifiable insanity.

ALICE: I'm not mad – something awful happened to me.

CHESHIRE CAT: Then you've got an excuse – Enjoy it. Why not?

ALICE: Because – it's not a fun kind of mad. It's not silly string, and – feeling a bit funny 'cause you've had too many Haribos.

Something really bad happened to me, and –

CHESHIRE CAT: Yes?

ALICE: You're smiling.

CHESHIRE CAT: I can't help it, I'm a Cheshire Cat.

ALICE: Something really bad happened to me and that's why.

CHESHIRE CAT: Bad like you climbed a tree and then couldn't get down again?

ALICE: Worse than that.

CHESHIRE CAT: Bad like your mouse toy went under a radiator and as hard as you stretched you couldn't pull it out?

ALICE: Much worse.

CHESHIRE CAT: Bad like someone's opened a can of tuna and you can't *believe* they're not going to give you any?

ALICE: Yeah, I don't think – Forget it, I've got to –

She looks at the signposts again.

It just doesn't make sense.

CHESHIRE CAT: Sweetness, what use is sense to anyone?

How adorable of you to want it to make sense. Nothing makes sense, love, just shut your eyes and accept it –

ALICE: But I don't know which way to go!

CHESHIRE CAT: You end up in the same place whichever sign you follow.

ALICE: Sorry?

CHESHIRE CAT: Whichever sign you follow, you end up in the same place.

ALICE: You mean – No, but one says Hatter and one says Hare.

CHESHIRE CAT: The Hare and the Hatter are having tea together – so if you follow the sign for the Hatter you get to the Hare and if you follow the sign for the Hare, you get to the Hatter.

ALICE: They point to the same place.

CHESHIRE CAT: Eventually.

ALICE: So if they all point to the same place, that must be the middle, mustn't it? That must be the Heart… Logically.

OK, good. It's not me that's mad, it's *here*, it's Wonderland. So if I was a mad person, what would I –

CHESHIRE CAT: I could keep you company. Ever run barefoot through a lollipop field?

ALICE: Look, I'm trying to –

CHESHIRE CAT: Ever heard the song of the rainbow bird?

ALICE: It's just I'm trying to think here –

CHESHIRE CAT: Do you know how they make stripy toothpaste?

ALICE: Look, I'm sure you're lovely but could you please go away.

CHESHIRE CAT: Harsh, my darling – I'm wounded.

ALICE: I'll rub your tummy once more if you go away after.

CHESHIRE CAT: How can I resist?

He stretches and ALICE rubs his tummy very briefly.

ALICE: OK, off you go now.

CHESHIRE CAT: No, you go.

ALICE: You go.

CHESHIRE CAT: No, you.

ALICE: Seriously. Really go.

CHESHIRE CAT: Yeah, alright I'm going.

Some people have no taste.

The CAT stalks off, his tail in the air.

ALICE: So – ok, so all I have to do is follow the signs, yeah?

She looks at one.

H R TEA.

ALICE walks in the way the sign seems to be pointing.

The signs will take me to the tea party at the centre of the universe and when I get there there'll probably be a door –

She looks at another sign.

H R TEA – this way.

ALICE walks in the direction that sign points to. She passes the POSTMAN, pulling the postbox behind him.

Hello.

POSTMAN: G'morning.

ALICE: So there'll be a door and I'll go through it and then I'll be back in my house.

ALICE stops, thinking. The POSTMAN also stops and starts to search through his postbox for something.

Back at home with all those people. And the funeral.

POSTMAN: Hang on a minute…

ALICE: What?

POSTMAN: Here it is – postcard for you.

The POSTMAN hands the postcard to ALICE and moves off.

ALICE: Yeah, thanks for the warning, by the way, about the Duchess.

ALICE looks down at the postcard and reads it.

'Don't forget what's in your pocket'

POSTMAN: Cheerio then.

ALICE: It doesn't say who it's from.

ALICE turns to the POSTMAN, but he's gone already.

'Don't forget what's in your pocket'? There's nothing in my pocket, it's all been eaten or given away as a prize or flipping confiscated or –

Oh.

ALICE pulls the other letter out of her pocket – the one the POSTMAN gave her earlier.

There was a letter. Divvy.

ALICE opens the letter. Unseen by her, the WONDERBAND arrange themselves close by.

OK, it's a poem or something.

She turns the letter over.

God, does no one sign their letters here?

She turns it back over and starts to read.

'Twas brillig, and the slithy toves
Did gyre and gimble in the wabe;

The WONDERBAND take over and start to sing. ALICE turns around, surprised.

WONDERBAND: *(Singing)*
'Twas brillig, and the slithy toves
Did gyre and gimble in the wabe;

ALICE closes the letter and the band stops abruptly.

She turns back to read it on her own but as soon as she opens it the band starts up again.

All mimsy were the borogoves,
And the mome raths outgrabe.

She closes it again and they stop.

She opens it very quickly and they start up, then she shuts it again after only a word or so.

ALICE turns back to the band.

ALICE: Sorry, can't I just read it myself –

WONDERBANDER: We've been paid to sing it, so –

ALICE: Yeah, I don't really like being sung to.

WONDERBANDER: If someone gives you a song you've got to listen.

WONDERBANDER: Please.

ALICE: Fine, OK, go on.

The WONDERBAND play her the whole poem.

WONDERBAND: *(Singing)*
'Twas brillig, and the slithy toves
Did gyre and gimble in the wabe;
All mimsy were the borogoves,
And the mome raths outgrabe.

"Beware the Jabberwock, my son!
The jaws that bite, the claws that catch!
Beware the Jubjub bird, and shun
The frumious Bandersnatch!"

He took his vorpal sword in hand:
Long time the manxome foe he sought–
So rested he by the Tumtum tree,
And stood awhile in thought.

And as in uffish thought he stood,
The Jabberwock, with eyes of flame,
Came whiffling through the tulgey wood,
And burbled as it came!

One, two! One, two! and through and through
The vorpal blade went snicker-snack!
He left it dead, and with its head
He went galumphing back.

"And hast thou slain the Jabberwock?
Come to my arms, my beamish boy!
O frabjous day! Callooh! Callay!"
He chortled in his joy.

'Twas brillig, and the slithy toves
Did gyre and gimble in the wabe;
All mimsy were the borogoves,
And the mome raths outgrabe.

The band stop. ALICE looks at the band, unsure what to do now.

ALICE: OK, could I have a translation, maybe?

One of the musicians comes towards ALICE with a clipboard.

WONDERBANDER: Sign here please.

ALICE: Why?

WONDERBANDER: To say you received the song.

ALICE signs the clipboard. The other band members start to move away.

ALICE: Hang on, you're not – Aren't you going to explain to me what it means?

WONDERBANDER: Not our job, love. We're just paid to sing it. Need a poetic licence if you want it explained.

ALICE looks at the piece of paper in her hand.

ALICE: But what's the point if you won't say who it's from and you won't tell me what it means?

WONDERBANDER: We don't write it, yeah, we just play it. Ask the Union.

The WONDERBAND leave.

ALICE: Is this supposed to distract me? Throw me off the path.

No, I was on a path, wasn't I – I was – I was going to the Hatter and the Hare, following the signposts to the –

ALICE looks around.

Following the signposts which have gone.

Maybe that means I'm here already – you don't have a sign pointing to Sheffield when you're in Sheffield, do you?

Oh.

ALICE sees the tea party and approaches quietly, not wanting them to see her yet.

HATTER is standing on a chair, regaling the HARE and the sleeping DORMOUSE with a story.

HATTER: So there am I, standing on a chair in front of the queen, no less –

HARE: No less, no more.

HATTER: The queen! Demanding I sing her a song.

HARE: Dear me, whatever did you do?

HATTER: I opened my mouth – and out came this, the most dreadful thing:

(Sings)
Twinkle twinkle little bat!
How I wonder what you're at!
Up above the world you fly,
Like a tea tray in the sky –

ALICE moves closer, staying out of sight.

HARE: A dreadful thing!

DORMOUSE: Twinkle twinkle…

HATTER: A very dreadful thing – I mixed the head voice and the chest voice. Unforgivable! And how was I to know the queen can't abide vibrato?

Stamped on my pocket watch in disgust, she did. I'm lucky to have escaped with my head.

DORMOUSE: Twinkle twinkle –

The HATTER holds up his watch to show the others.

HATTER: Six o'clock, always six o'clock and nothing to be done about it.

The HATTER looks at his watch.

Look at that – time for tea.

He climbs down off his chair. ALICE tries to duck out of sight, but it's too late – he sees her.

Wait – who's there –

HARE: Who is it, who's there?

HATTER: A spy –

The HARE quickly takes a pot of jam from the table top and hides it underneath.

HARE: A spy – good gracious!

ALICE: I'm not a spy – I promise, I'm just looking for –

Are you the Hatter and the Hare?

HATTER: She's an emissary from the queen.

ALICE: I'm not, I promise.

HARE: Prove it.

ALICE: I'm just looking for the middle, the centre. Of, um, Wonderland. Is there, like a door here somewhere?

HARE: A door? A door?

HATTER: When is a door not a door?

ALICE: Um, when it's ajar. That's really old.

DORMOUSE: A jar of jam.

HARE: No jam! No jam!

HATTER: Are you sure you're not the queen's spy? You do look awfully like her.

HARE: She does look awfully like her.

HATTER: Two arms, two legs, nose right in the middle of your face like that.

ALICE: I've never met the bloody queen!

HARE: Nasty, vicious temper she's got.

HATTER: Don't they teach you manners? At *spy school?*

The HATTER and HARE advance on ALICE and back her into a chair. The HARE arranges a lamp so that it's shining directly into ALICE's face.

ALICE: School's not supposed to teach you manners, that's for your parents – school's for maths and stuff.

HATTER: Maths, you say – let's see, shall we?

HARE: Can you do Addition?

HATTER: What's one and one and one and one and one and one and one and one and one and one?

ALICE: I don't know, I lost count.

HARE: She can't do Addition.

HATTER: Can you do Subtraction? Take nine from eight.

ALICE: Minus one!

HATTER: Yours is one what?

HARE: She can't do Substraction.

HATTER: Can you do Division? Divide a loaf by a knife – what's the answer to *that?*

ALICE: Um,

HATTER: Bread-and-butter, of course.

HARE: She can't do sums a bit.

HATTER: Do you know your ABC?

ALICE: Yeah, I'm not a baby.

HARE: I can read words of one letter. It's true, I can.

HATTER: Do you know languages? What's the French for 'ecky thump'?

ALICE: Ecky thump isn't even proper English. I don't know what it means.

The HATTER moves away from ALICE, looking at her carefully.

HATTER: The queen's spy would know what it means.

HARE: Meaning?

HATTER: She's quite safe.

The HATTER looks at his watch.

Look at that – six o'clock. Time for tea.

The HATTER and the HARE move back towards the table.

Cup of tea, old chap?

ALICE: Am I right, though – is this the middle?

HARE: Tis the place where all roads meet. Have some wine, dear boy.

ALICE: Um. Thank you.

ALICE comes closer, looks at the table.

There isn't any wine.

HARE: More's the pity.

ALICE: If there isn't a door, is there a chute or something, maybe –

Like a magic portal or –

HATTER: Have some more tea, dear boy.

ALICE: I haven't had any yet. So I can't have *more*, can I?

HATTER: You can't have *less*, it's very easy to have *more* than none.

ALICE: If I'm in the right place, then what do I do? Make a wish and touch the teapot?

HATTER: Talks to himself – mad, you see.

ALICE: I'm actually a girl, by the way.

HATTER: You see what I mean?

ALICE: Maybe I just sit and wait for a bit and then something turns into a door or –

ALICE sits down at the table. The HARE pulls a cup out of a large jelly and pours a cup of tea for ALICE.

HARE: Nice cup of tea and no need to worry about anything.

ALICE: Could I have a bit of bread and some jam?

HATTER: Jam?

HARE: Jam?

DORMOUSE: A jar of jam.

HATTER: There's no jam here, dear boy.

HARE: All jam property of the queen!

HATTER: Anyone found with contraband jam will be beheaded!

HARE: With his own teaspoon!

HATTER: Have some bread and butter. WITHOUT jam.

HARE: It's Wonderloaf.

ALICE: Is it all types of jam?

DORMOUSE: Strawberry jam, apricot jam…

HATTER: Are we sure she isn't an emissary from the queen?

HARE: A what?

DORMOUSE: Blackcurrant jam…

HATTER: A *spy*, remember?

DORMOUSE: Gooseberry jam...

ALICE: What about traffic jam?

HATTER: See, this is a test.

DORMOUSE: Rhubarb jam...

ALICE: Or paper jam?

HARE: *Paper* jam?

ALICE: You know: 'Warning: Paper Jam".

HARE: We know of no such thing.

HATTER: All jam property of the queen and that's all there is to it.

DORMOUSE: Damson, greengage...

ALICE: Why does the queen need all the jam?

HATTER: For the tarts, of course.

HARE: Only the queen can make tarts.

HATTER: By which we mean only the queen is *clever* enough to make tarts.

DORMOUSE: Loganberry...

ALICE: Jam tarts? Jam tarts are easy.

HATTER: She's luring us. This is a trap, don't fall into it.

I was a hatter, you know. Oh yes. They came from miles around for my hats.

One blow from the queen's stiletto and goodbye to all that.

DORMOUSE: Ginger jam...

ALICE: She kicked you?

HATTER: She might as well have.

The HATTER shows ALICE his watch.

DORMOUSE: Victoria plum...

ALICE: She stamped on your watch?

HATTER: I made her *very* angry.

DORMOUSE: Quince…

The DORMOUSE falls asleep.

ALICE: She doesn't sound very nice, the queen.

The HATTER and HARE gasp at her outspokenness.

When was this?

HATTER: Last March – just before he went mad.

The HATTER shakes his pocket watch, looking at it.

What day of the month is it?

ALICE: The seventeenth.

HATTER: Two weeks wrong. I told you butter wouldn't suit the works.

ALICE: You put *butter* in it?

HARE: It was the best butter.

HATTER: Yes, but some crumbs must have got in as well. You shouldn't have put it in with the bread knife.

Oh look – six o'clock: time for tea!

HARE: Move round, move round!

ALICE: Haven't you just had your tea?

The HATTER shows her the watch.

HATTER: If it's six o'clock, it's tea time.

ALICE: So this thing with the queen happened last March and you've been having tea ever since, you've been stuck.

HARE: My head hurts.

ALICE: You've probably had too much caffeine.

The HATTER gives the HARE his watch.

HATTER: Here –

The HARE holds the watch to his forehead.

Time's a great healer.

What say we change the subject? I vote the young chap tells us a story.

ALICE: I'm actually a girl, I did say –

HARE: I'd love a story.

ALICE: I don't know any.

HATTER: Then the Dormouse shall.

ALICE: Could really do with that magic portal right now…

HARE: Wake up, Dormouse!

The HATTER pours some tea onto the DORMOUSE's nose and he wakes up, spluttering.

HATTER: We demand a story!

HARE: Oh please oh please.

DORMOUSE: Alright, but you'll definitely not like it.

The DORMOUSE readies himself to tell the story, clearing his throat etc. ALICE uses the moment to reach for a piece of bread and butter.

Once upon a time there was a…

The DORMOUSE nearly dozes off, then wakes up again with a start.

Once upon a time there was a…

HATTER: Spit it out quickly, before you fall asleep again, there's a good chap.

DORMOUSE: Once upon a time there was a little boy and his name was Joe –

ALICE stops, with the piece of bread half way to her mouth.

ALICE: Joe?

DORMOUSE: Joe.

ALICE: My brother Joe?

Is this what I'm here for? Are you going to tell me
something important about Joe?

DORMOUSE: His name was Joe and he lived at the bottom of
a well.

HARE: Well well here's a story, eh?

ALICE: No, he lived in Broomhill, surely?

DORMOUSE: He lived at the bottom of a well.

ALICE puts the piece of bread and butter down.

ALICE: OK, is this some kind of code – like a whatsitcalled,
like we did at school, um – If I solve the riddle, I get my
door, yes?

HATTER: What did he live on?

ALICE: A metaphor.

DORMOUSE: He lived on treacle.

HARE: Metaphor. Met her for what?

ALICE: Treacle?

DORMOUSE: Treacle.

ALICE: You can't live on treacle, you'd be sick.

DORMOUSE: So he was. Very sick.

ALICE: Why was he at the bottom of a well?

I don't know any wells. Unless you mean like Forge Dam,
or Abbeydale Hamlet or something –

DORMOUSE: It was a treacle-well.

HATTER: No such thing!

ALICE: OK, so is the well – is that a metaphor for the, um, car
crash, or –

Not very *good* metaphor, is it? What does the treacle stand
for? Is that me, or. Did Joe have a sister?

DORMOUSE: If you can't listen properly, you'd better finish the story for yourself.

ALICE: No, please go on – please. Tell me about Joe.

DORMOUSE: He was learning to draw, you know –

ALICE: What did he draw?

The DORMOUSE pauses for a moment.

DORMOUSE: Treacle.

HATTER: You can't draw treacle.

DORMOUSE: If you can draw water out of a water-well, you can draw treacle out of a treacle-well.

Stories are so tiring.

HATTER: I want a clean cup! Move round, move round!

ALICE: Wait – please finish the story.

HARE: Move round, move round!

ALICE: Please, this is really important.

ALICE has to collude with the moving-round, but during the movement, the DORMOUSE falls asleep again. ALICE pokes him.

Tell me what the treacle means, what the drawing means –

Hello? Hello? What about the story?

ALICE shakes the DORMOUSE by the shoulder, trying to rouse him.

He wakes up and looks at her.

DORMOUSE: I wasn't asleep, you know.

ALICE: Please tell the rest of the story – about Joe?

The DORMOUSE shakes his head confused.

DORMOUSE: Joe…

ALICE: Who lived in a well?

DORMOUSE: Joe…

ALICE: A treacle well?

DORMOUSE: Treacle, strawberry jam –

ALICE: Right. This is just nonsense, isn't it? You're just spouting rubbish.

The DORMOUSE shakes his head, then falls asleep with the effort.

DORMOUSE: Twinkle twinkle twinkle twinkle…

HATTER: Look at that – six o'clock. Time for tea.

HARE: Move round, move round!

ALICE: You're all broken, you're stuck.

HATTER: You must have something to eat.

ALICE: I don't want to eat anything I'm very upset.

The HATTER holds his watch towards ALICE.

HATTER: Time's a great healer, you know.

ALICE: Stupid wild goose chase – like yeah, go find the middle and then it's all full of mentals like you lot –

HATTER: Look: six o'clock – time for tea.

ALICE: For god's sake.

HARE: It was the best butter – tea's mashed!

HATTER: And then there I am, standing on a chair in front of the queen, no less –

HARE: The queen of Hearts!

HATTER: The very one…

ALICE: The queen of *Hearts*?

HATTER: Demanding I sing her a song.

The HATTER and the HARE continue their dialogue, having got back to the beginning of their eternal loop. ALICE moves away, thinking.

ALICE: The queen is the queen of *Hearts*? Like on a pack of cards?

Oh my god – that's what it means – the queen of Hearts. 'Go right to the Heart' means I have to go and see the queen, right, surely?

The queen of Hearts!

Queens live in castles, no palaces – did the duchess mention a palace?

There must be a palace, right? So where's that?

Find the palace find the palace…

A teenage BOY (14 or 15.) appears, wearing chef whites and wheeling a strange contraption in front of him. A little like a hostess trolley, it has a fan and a conveyor belt, along which are passing a batch of strawberry jam tarts, and underneath this, a sort of cupboard.

ALICE goes over to him.

Excuse me?

BOY: Alright?

ALICE: Is there um, is there a palace here?

BOY: Well *duh.*

ALICE: Pardon?

BOY: Course there's a palace, where d'you think I work?

ALICE: OK, can you tell me where it is?

BOY: God, d'you know nothing?

ALICE: You hum it and I'll tell you.

BOY: *What?*

ALICE: Sorry, my dad says that.

Sorry, could you just basically tell me where the palace is and then I'll go away.

BOY: It's over there.

A GIRL around the same age as the boy appears. She has an armful of red and white roses. The BOY's attention immediately switches away from ALICE.

ALICE: OK, thank you.

BOY: Whatever.

(To the girl.) Got enough flowers, haven't you?

GIRL: That your best line? They're *roses.*

BOY: Someone give them to you, did they?

GIRL: For the queen. Didn't know if she wanted red or white.

Gardener just said 'roses'.

BOY: She'll want red ones.

GIRL: What, she's your girlfriend, is she?

BOY: She always wants red ones. Ask anyone.

GIRL: What am I going to do with all the white ones, then?

BOY: Keep them for yourself. I'd let you, if I was gardener.

They move off a little, talking closely. Their conversation continues softly under the next:

Unseen by the BOY and GIRL, a man climbs out from the cupboard under the tart-cooling trolley. This is the KNAVE OF HEARTS. He's dressed like a burglar, and has a bag slung over his shoulder. He takes a tart from the top of the trolley and puts it in his bag, then dashes out of sight.

The BOY comes back towards the trolley to wind up the fan.

ALICE: Excuse me –

BOY: And actually chef's said my knife skills were pretty amazing, you know, for my age. He said if I carry on like this, he'll put me on jam in a few years time, he can see me having a career in puddings, he said.

ALICE: Sorry, but –

BOY: *(To Alice.)* It's over there, I told you.

GIRL: Rory's already on puddings.

BOY: He said that, did he, that he's already on puddings?

During this, the KNAVE steals another tart, and again is seen by ALICE, but not the BOY. It happens again a number of times.

I mean yeah, he is, if by 'on puddings' you mean pudding *assistant.* Cause that's as far as he can go, actually, in that job, it's a dead end. Unless you've got training, experience on all the other stations. Pudding assistant's the highest you can go unless you've got the basic grounding in everything else, so –

Basically Rory's on a path to eternal skivvitude and he doesn't even know it.

ALICE: Excuse me, but there's a man –

BOY: D'you know you're really annoying? I told you, the palace is over there.

ALICE: Yes, but someone's –

BOY: *(To the girl.)* By the way, are you going to the croquet?

GIRL: Maybe, why?

ALICE: No, fine, ignore me, carry on.

BOY: Just they've given me a second ticket, so –

GIRL: Yeah, I've got a ticket.

ALICE: There's a man stealing your cakes, yeah?

BOY: But is it in the royal stand?

GIRL: No.

ALICE: Hello?

BOY: Stick with me, princess.

ALICE: I mean he's being pretty obvious.

BOY: They don't let just anyone do the tart cooling, you know. Responsibility.

GIRL: What tarts?

BOY: These. Tarts.

The BOY turns to look at the trolley, but there are no tarts left, they've all been taken.

GIRL: Like I say, what tarts?

BOY: No no no no no – no no no – oh my – They were there, where've they gone –

The BOY panics.

No no no no no I am in massive trouble. This is Jamageddon, they're going to kill me…

He runs off with the trolley, and the GIRL hurries after him.

GIRL: It's not your fault, though…

The KNAVE comes towards ALICE, threateningly.

ALICE: It's not very nice, you know, taking other people's cake –

KNAVE: You saw nothing, right?

ALICE: I saw you take all those – that poor boy, it's not fair to –

The KNAVE comes right up to ALICE and takes her chin in his hand.

KNAVE: You didn't see anything.

If you tell them what you saw, I'll kill you.

Got that?

ALICE nods, speechless. He leaves, stealthily.

ALICE is left alone.

Interval.

ACT TWO

The Queen's Croquet Ground. A number of young WONDERLANDERS are playing croquet on the lawn, watched by two COMMENTATORS in their own mobile commentary box.

ALICE sits at the edge of the lawn, with the DUCHESS next to her.

COMMENTATOR 1: And that cracking shot concludes our warm-up match from the Junior Wonderlanders Croquet League.

COMMENTATOR 2: Stars of the future there…

COMMENTATOR 1: Yes indeed. And on their way to the podium now for the medals presentation.

COMMENTATOR 2: Who knows, one day these youngsters may find themselves being presented with a medal by the queen herself.

COMMENTATOR 1: What a proud day that would be.

DUCHESS: Isn't it exciting, dolly?

ALICE: What?

DUCHESS: To be here. Today.

ALICE: I um – I don't quite know how I got here.

DUCHESS: I'm like that, I forget things all the time.

ALICE: I mean I was just talking to that scary man and now I'm – Now I'm here.

Sorry, where am I exactly?

DUCHESS: Silly dolly. You're at the queen's croquet ground.

ALICE: The queen of Hearts?

DUCHESS: Aren't you more excited than you've ever been? A game of croquet and then tea.

ALICE: I don't really know anything about croquet.

DUCHESS: Gosh dolly, don't say that anywhere near her majesty – the queen's mad for croquet.

ALICE: Is the queen here?

DUCHESS: She'll be here any minute, for the big match. Do you really mean to tell me you've never played croquet?

ALICE: It's a bit old-fashioned where I come from.

DUCHESS: Darling dolly, come over here and let me show you.

They go towards a rack of flamingos and a bucket of hedgehogs.

ALICE: Um, look, there's something I should tell you.

DUCHESS: Don't tell me – you think I'm so much calmer since you last saw me, my skin's looking so much better…

ALICE: Yeah, it's just – You know the baby?

DUCHESS: The little pig.

ALICE: Yes.

The DUCHESS looks at a number of flamingos.

DUCHESS: You'll need one of these.

ALICE: Thing is, it turned out it was actually a pig.

DUCHESS: Yes, I know. Horrid little thing, caterwauling all the –

Here you are – this might be the right size.

The DUCHESS hands ALICE the flamingo. ALICE doesn't know how to hold it.

ALICE: The thing is, um, I'm terribly sorry, but –

DUCHESS: No, that's too short.

ALICE: I'm everso sorry but I'm afraid it ran away.

DUCHESS: What about this one?

The DUCHESS hands her another flamingo.

What ran away?

ALICE: The pig. The pigbaby. I'm really sorry. It just ran off, so –

DUCHESS: Oh don't worry about that, dolly. Getting that baby off my hands was the best thing I ever did – I can't tell you how much better I feel – calmer, more adjusted, freer, less tense – so much less tense, I was carrying all this tension in my neck, in my shoulders –

No dolly, you're holding it the wrong way up.

ALICE: Um, OK.

DUCHESS: And you must greet it nicely.

ALICE: Sorry?

DUCHESS: Say hello.

ALICE: Um, hello. Flamingo.

FLAMINGO: Mr Flamingo if you don't mind.

DUCHESS: You've to be very polite or it won't hit when you want it to.

ALICE: Um, sorry. Mr Flamingo.

FLAMINGO: That's better.

DUCHESS: Bad-tempered things, flamingos, but you have to humour them.

FLAMINGO: I heard that.

DUCHESS: Isn't this fun? Now, you need a hedgehog as well.

That's the other good thing about losing the silly baby – now the queen will surely have me back. As soon as she sees me she'll – You don't think she's only got me here to make up the numbers or something, do you?

ALICE: I'm sure not.

The DUCHESS has picked a hedgehog for ALICE.

DUCHESS: Here's a good beginner's one, try this. Just give it a little tap with the flamingo.

ALICE: Isn't that cruel?

DUCHESS: No no, they love it.

HEDGEHOG: Hello, my name's Roger and I'm going to be your hedgehog for today – any questions at all, don't hesitate to ask.

Now feel free to hit me as hard as you like – I am a professional. Though I would ask you please to avoid the facial area as I need that for my modelling contracts.

ALICE: Modelling?

HEDGEHOG: I'm wasted here, quite frankly.

DUCHESS: Go on, dolly – have a go.

HEDGEHOG: So I roll up like this and then you hit me.

ALICE: With the flamingo.

FLAMINGO: *Mr* Flamingo.

HEDGEHOG: And then you try to get me through that little arch there, OK.

ALICE has a go. The HEDGEHOG yelps each time he's hit.

Eeep! Thank you.

DUCHESS: Very good. Keep going.

You do think the queen will receive me today, don't you? Just have to make sure I pick the right moment –

A fanfare.

Oh dolly, she's coming, she's coming.

The DUCHESS drags ALICE off the pitch.

COMMENTATOR 1: If you've just joined us we're reporting from the annual All – Wonderland Croquet Tournament, in the presence of her majesty the queen, croquet's greatest fan.

COMMENTATOR 2: And of course his majesty the king.

COMMENTATOR 1: The king, yes, and her majesty the queen looking as radiant as ever – you know, it's a wonder to me to think that those delicate hands were up until last night hard at work baking tarts, and yet now here she is, quite serene, not a dusting of flour or a spot of jam in sight.

She is, truly, the Queen of Hearts.

COMMENTATOR 2: And what a tea we shall all have later.

COMMENTATOR 1: The white rabbit there, attending to every royal whim in his usual indispensable way, the model of discretion.

ALICE: *(To DUCHESS.)* Does the White Rabbit work for the queen?

COMMENTATOR 2: What secrets must those ears have heard, eh?

COMMENTATOR 1: Yes indeed.

ALICE: If he works for the queen that must mean I'm in the right place, mustn't it?

COMMENTATOR 2: Not um, not bad secrets, I mean –

COMMENTATOR 1: The queen now rising from her royal seat to address the crowd – a reverent hush, if you please.

The QUEEN stands up.

ALICE looks at the QUEEN properly for the first time.

ALICE: She looks like my mum!

DUCHESS: Shhh.

QUEEN: Most dear, most loyal, most delicious subjects.

ALICE: She sounds like my mum, too –

QUEEN: It is with great pleasure that you would like to thank me for laying on such a magnificent spectacle this afternoon, and for the love and fidelity that you enjoy. From me.

ALICE: This means I'm definitely in the right place.

DUCHESS: Really, dolly, you ought to be quiet.

QUEEN: I think we can all agree that there is no-one in all Wonderland more wonderful than me, and for that you are of course, profoundly grateful. From the bottom of your hearts.

ALICE: I should go and speak to her then maybe she can click her fingers or her shoes or something and get me out of here.

ALICE steps over the rope at the side of the pitch to try to move towards the QUEEN, but before she's covered any distance, a match OFFICIAL swoops in and stops her.

OFFICIAL: Sorry miss, you can't go over there.

ALICE: But I need to speak to my –

OFFICIAL: Come on, we don't want any trouble – off the green, please.

ALICE: But I want to talk to the queen.

OFFICIAL: Only players allowed to approach the queen, miss.

QUEEN: My husband and I were remarking only the other day how lucky you are to be ruled by such a just, reasonable, compassionate queen as me –

There's a shout from an unseen WONDERLANDER in the crowd.

WONDERLANDER: Tell us about the tarts!

QUEEN: Who said that? Off with his head!

The KING comes closer to the QUEEN's side.

KING: Beheadings later, my dear – Please continue, we're hanging on every word.

The QUEEN composes herself and continues.

QUEEN: I simply cannot tell you how pleased you are to be here, in the presence of. Me are happy to invite you all – or those of you still in possession of your heads by that point – to a croquet tea at which my home made tarts will be served to the most deserving among you.

But before that – to the match. What a happy coincidence that croquet, my favourite sport, is also the favourite sport of all Wonderlanders everywhere. And what an exciting game me will have today – a champion, undefeated for twenty-five matches, and an unknown challenger. Who among you is brave enough to take on this quest for glory?

The QUEEN looks at the crowd. No-one volunteers.

I SAID – who among you is brave enough to take on the challenge?

ALICE: Why won't anyone volunteer?

DUCHESS: No one could defeat the champion. He's –

QUEEN: Never mind that the last challenger had to have a hedgehog removed from his buttocks – he was right as rain in no time.

Come on, Wonderland. Where's your lust for adventure?

Still no volunteers.

I WANT TO WATCH SOME CROQUET.

If no one volunteers then off with everyone's head. Off with his head, and her head, and his head and his head and off with their heads over there and…

ALICE: If I play, I'll get to meet the queen, right?

DUCHESS: You play?

ALICE looks at her HEDGEHOG and FLAMINGO.

ALICE: What d'you think, guys?

HEDGEHOG: No no no I'm scared, he's scary.

FLAMINGO: Do you know, I can't today, I've got to go to the chiropodist.

ALICE: Come on, let's be brave, let's do it.

ALICE goes to the match official.

I'd like to be the challenger, please.

OFFICIAL: Are you sure?

QUEEN: … and your head and your head and –

OFFICIAL: Your majesty – we have a challenger.

ALICE steps forward. The QUEEN looks her up and down with a flicker of recognition, then claps her hands, delighted.

The crowd breathes a sigh of relief.

QUEEN: Bring out the champion!

The crowd goes wild as the champion (wearing a helmet with a face-cage) is carried in, triumphant, and does a pre-emptive lap of honour.

COMMENTATOR 1: The crowd going suitably loopy there for the entrance of the All-Wonderland Croquet champion.

COMMENTATOR 2: And we've just been passed some statistics about today's challenger – never been known to win a tournament, never to our knowledge even handled a flamingo.

COMMENTATOR 1: Could this be the shortest game in the history of this venerable championship?

The champion takes off his mask and snarls at the crowd who squeal with delight.

ALICE recognises him.

ALICE: That's the man – that's the man I saw! *He's* the champion?

FLAMINGO: The Knave of Hearts.

ALICE: But he can't be – I saw him –

FLAMINGO: Never been beaten. He's the queen's favourite.

HEDGEHOG: Gosh, the things he can do with a hedgehog…

The KNAVE, having finished snarling at the crowd, advances on ALICE, menacingly. She stands with her flamingo lowered, trying to be brave. He circles her, then comes close and looks her in the eye, challengingly.

He puts his helmet back on and smacks it down on the top of his head – he's ready to play. The crowd whoop and cheer. The KNAVE backs away from ALICE, and goes to select a flamingo from a rack displayed to him by the OFFICIAL.

FLAMINGO: Oooh – ahh – the blood's all rushing to my head – ahhh –

HEDGEHOG: You mustn't leave him upside down for too long – the blood all rushes to his head.

ALICE: I'm so sorry.

ALICE lifts the FLAMINGO to an upright position.

FLAMINGO: Oh yes, that's much bet –

The FLAMINGO faints, going floppy in ALICE's arms.

ALICE: Oh god, is he alright?

HEDGEHOG: He'll come round any minute.

The FLAMINGO is still.

Any minute now…

ALICE: Is he going to be OK to play?

COMMENTATOR 1: The Knave now kneeling at the feet of his patron, her majesty the queen who is –

COMMENTATOR 2: We think –

COMMENTATOR 1: Yes yes, she's about to give him the royal hedgehog to play with.

COMMENTATOR 2: An honour indeed.

The QUEEN gives the KING a signal and he opens a small wooden box with a golden hedgehog inside it. He offers the hedgehog to the KNAVE, who takes it and bows to the QUEEN. She waves, regally, then gives her husband another signal.

KING: Let's play croquet!

FLAMINGO: Come on then, let's get on with it.

HEDGEHOG: It's your shot first.

ALICE walks to the first hoop.

COMMENTATOR 1: Our challenger now coming to the starting position to take the first shot.

ALICE puts her HEDGEHOG down on the floor.

Let's go in for a closer look.

The COMMENTATORS wheel themselves towards ALICE and watch her intently.

COMMENTATOR 2: The concentration on the challenger's face – what must she be feeling at this moment right now?

ALICE takes the shot, and it gets almost to the hoop.

COMMENTATOR 1: Not a bad shot there from the challenger, but will it be enough?

The KNAVE steps onto the pitch and places his hedgehog in the starting position.

COMMENTATOR 2: Here we go now – the Knave getting ready for the shot –

He knocks his hedgehog towards the hoop, but it seems to be going off course.

KNAVE: Look up there!

Everyone except ALICE looks up in the sky where the KNAVE is pointing. He runs to his hedgehog, and taps it with his foot so that it's going through the hoop just as everyone looks back down again.

Sorry, thought I saw something.

COMMENTATOR 1: Classic shot. A player at the very top of his game.

ALICE: He was cheating!

KING: Action replay!

Everyone goes backwards to where they were for the KNAVE's shot, then he plays it in slow motion as if it had gone through the hoop perfectly. The QUEEN claps with delight.

ALICE: That's not what happened!

COMMENTATOR 2: A triumphant first hoop for the Knave.

COMMENTATOR 1: Time for the challenger's next shot – can she get through that first hoop at last?

ALICE hits her hedgehog and it goes through the first hoop.

COMMENTATOR 1: Yes, keeping herself in a steady second place, there.

ALICE: Yeah, OK, I'm trying my best.

The KNAVE steps up to take his next shot. It gets a good way towards the second hoop, but doesn't go through it.

The KNAVE makes a frustrated sound and smacks his flamingo's head on the floor. The crowd inhales sharply.

COMMENTATOR 2: The Knave showing some frustration there.

COMMENTATOR 1: The point at which he'd usually call for a new –

KNAVE: New flamingo!

COMMENTATOR 1: Yes, he's calling for a new flamingo now.

The OFFICIAL hands the KNAVE another flamingo and the KNAVE hands the OFFICIAL his old one.

COMMENTATOR 2: Let's hope this helps him onto a happier footing.

COMMENTATOR 1: What's the challenger's going to do now?

ALICE takes her shot. It looks like it'll go through the second hoop, but then the KNAVE puts down a bowl of bread and milk at the side of the hoop, and the hedgehog goes towards that instead.

QUEEN: Well played!

ALICE: That's not fair.

ALICE goes up to the official.

He's giving my hedgehog food – that's cheating.

The OFFICIAL looks towards the QUEEN. The QUEEN nods to the KING.

KING: Play on!

The KNAVE takes his shot and his hedgehog sails through the hoop.

COMMENTATOR 1: Beautiful.

COMMENTATOR 2: Liquid croquet.

COMMENTATOR 1: That's the kind of shot that gets me out of bed in the morning, I have to say.

The QUEEN claps and nods to the KING again.

KING: Free shot to the Knave!

ALICE: What? No!

COMMENTATOR 2: A well-deserved bonus now for the Knave –

The KNAVE takes his free shot and his hedgehog goes towards the third hoop, but not through it.

Not a bad shot, but not his best.

QUEEN: Free shot to the Knave!

COMMENTATOR 2: The queen herself calling for a free shot.

COMMENTATOR 1: Royal prerogative in action there from croquet's greatest fan.

The KNAVE hits his hedgehog and it goes through the third hoop. The QUEEN and the crowd all cheer. ALICE looks on, helpless.

QUEEN: Hurrah! Free shot!

The KNAVE hits his hedgehog towards the fourth hoop.

Free shot!

COMMENTATOR 2: And another free shot…

The QUEEN calls for as many free shots as it takes for the KNAVE to get his hedgehog through the fourth hoop.

The KNAVE pants, showing some fatigue.

COMMENTATOR 1: A brilliant run for the Knave, bringing him tantalisingly close to the winner's post.

KING: Time Out!

COMMENTATOR 1: The king calling time out now, giving the players a well-earned rest.

The KNAVE goes to sit in a chair and is surrounded by attendants who mop his brow, feed him drinks and generally gee him up.

COMMENTATOR 2: While we're waiting for play to resume, why don't we read out a few of your birthday messages?

COMMENTATOR 1: Yes, I've a card here saying happy birthday Betsy from all your friends in Wonderland Border Control…

ALICE: This is stupid – I might as well give up.

HEDGEHOG: I'm sorry, I'm a sucker for a bit of bread and milk.

ALICE: If he's going to play like that, cheating all the time. I can't beat it. And anyway, everyone wants him to win.

FLAMINGO: No one beats the Knave of Hearts.

ALICE: Yeah, I can see why. No one gets a fair run.

COMMENTATOR 1: And here's another of your messages, though I'm not sure I quite understand this one.

COMMENTATOR 2: What does it say?

COMMENTATOR 1: 'Alice. Alice. Alice. Has anyone seen Alice. I can't find Alice. I've looked everywhere. D'you think she's run off somewhere? Alice. Alice.'

COMMENTATOR 2: Seems to be for someone called Alice.

ALICE: I'm Alice, that's me.

COMMENTATOR 1: Sure it makes perfect sense to someone out there.

FLAMINGO: Who was it from?

HEDGEHOG: Sounded a bit worried.

ALICE: My dad – Dad? Mum? I'm here – I'm trying to get back.

If they can send a message, they must be close, mustn't they? I must be near the end.

OK, guys. Let's win this so I can get home.

FLAMINGO: Win this? How can we win this? No-one beats the –

ALICE: Yeah, you said.

But wouldn't it be amazing if we did beat him? Why should he get away with it, playing like that? He smacked that poor flamingo's head really hard.

FLAMINGO: That was my cousin Harold.

ALICE: Let's do it for Harold.

HEDGEHOG: But how can we do it?

ALICE: I don't know, but why don't we – Give it our best shot. You just have to do the best you can with what you've got, don't you?

FLAMINGO: My best shot...

ALICE: *Literally* your best shot. D'you want to be the kind of flamingo that just gives in when things get difficult?

FLAMINGO: No. No, right, come on then. For Harold.

ALICE: Roger? Who's to say you can't fly if you want to?

HEDGEHOG: Yes. Yes, you're right. I'm a champion in the making. Let's play the game of our lives.

ALICE: This is so massively cheesy it's *got* to work.

KING: Play on!

COMMENTATOR 1: The King calling for the game to be resumed there.

COMMENTATOR 2: If you've just joined us, the Knave looks to be only one shot away from a resounding victory.

COMMENTATOR 1: One final consolation shot for the challenger first.

COMMENTATOR 2: And there she is, flamingo at the ready – what's that expression on her face, would you say?

COMMENTATOR 1: If I didn't know better I'd say it was –

COMMENTATOR 2: Yes?

COMMENTATOR 1: I'd say it was *determination*.

ALICE steels herself and takes the shot.

By sheer force of will, Roger the Hedgehog goes through the third hoop, through the fourth then turns a corner to hit the winners post. The crowd gasp in amazement.

COMMENTATOR 2: That's it! That's it! The challenger has won the match!

COMMENTATOR 1: The Knave of Hearts *and* the laws of physics taking an absolute pasting there. What a game.

COMMENTATOR 2: Who'd have thought at the beginning of today that by the end of today the world would look as very different as it looks now at the end of today.

COMMENTATOR 1: Yes indeed. A new All-Wonderland Croquet champion.

COMMENTATOR 2: Won it fair and square.

COMMENTATOR 1: And doesn't the Knave of Hearts look cross about it.

The KNAVE storms off in a huff.

COMMENTATOR 2: Yes, he'll be kicking himself tonight. The challenger now approaching the podium to receive her medal from her majesty the queen.

COMMENTATOR 1: A great honour for any citizen of Wonderland.

COMMENTATOR 2: Seconds away from coming face to face with her majesty.

ALICE: Hello.

QUEEN: I beg your pardon.

ALICE: Hi. I mean, here I am, so –

QUEEN: Are you addressing me?

ALICE: Mission accomplished, here I am. Mum.

QUEEN: Mum?

ALICE: OK, no, sorry – just you look a lot like my mum, so –

WHITE RABBIT: The medal, your majesty.

The WHITE RABBIT hands the queen the gold winner's medal.

ALICE: Hi.

WHITE RABBIT: Hello?

The OFFICIAL comes over to the WHITE RABBIT and whispers in his ear.

One moment.

The WHITE RABBIT steps away to speak to the official in private. The QUEEN hangs the medal around ALICE's neck.

QUEEN: I wanted the knave to win. He's my favourite.

ALICE: Yeah, I'm sorry. But I needed to speak to you. And the Duchess sort of said that the only way I could do that was to play croquet and get presented to you at the end.

QUEEN: The Duchess said this? The Duchess?

ALICE: I've done everything I was supposed to do, yeah? So now I'm ready to go back, because I think my dad is kind of worried about where I am.

QUEEN: The Duchess!

ALICE: Look, I'm happy to hand the medal back and give it to the Knave if you want to for some kind of technicality because I want to go home really, more than I wanted to win at the croquet.

QUEEN: Give it to me, then.

ALICE takes the medal off her neck and hands it back to the QUEEN.

The WHITE RABBIT returns and goes close to the queen.

WHITE RABBIT: Your majesty –

He whispers in her ear. The QUEEN suddenly shrieks.

QUEEN: Stolen! My tarts? Who stole my tarts?

That's it – No more croquet! Whoever stole the tarts will lose his head!

The whole crowd quakes with fear.

Out of my way!

The QUEEN goes to leave. As she is doing so, the DUCHESS steps into her path.

DUCHESS: Your majesty – may I say how delightful it is to me to be back at court and back in your –

QUEEN: Get out of my way, idiot!

DUCHESS: But your majesty – You're my best friend!

The QUEEN leaves, with the DUCHESS pursuing her.

ALICE: No – wait – please – I need to speak to you –

The WONDERLANDERS hurriedly pack away the croquet ground – rolling the lawn up and carrying it off, wheeling out the QUEEN's podium etc… ALICE tries to get to the QUEEN, but is thwarted every time by people standing in front of her.

No – please – please come back –

ALICE is left alone as everything and everyone gets packed away.

The big door clanks shut behind her and ALICE shouts with frustration.

No no NO!

I don't know what to do I don't know what to do.

I mean what else do you bloody want me to do?

I've played the stupid game, I've done the Heart thing – it's not a place, I've tried that, and it's not a person I mean I'm running out of options here, I'm struggling for any kind of idea at all. I've tried to talk to all these mental people but d'you know what? *They're all mental!* Nobody's given me anything that's even remotely useful – what, a stupid piece-of-nonsense poem and I'm supposed to go 'oh yeah, eureka, I know exactly what to do now'.

ALICE hears a voice from another world.

MUM: Has anyone seen Alice?

ALICE: Mum?

DAD: We can't find her anywhere.

ALICE: I'm here!

DAD: Have you checked the attic?

ALICE: The attic's Joe's room, I can't go in there.

MUM: I don't know, I can't go in there.

DAD: She's probably just hiding somewhere.

MUM: Maybe she's gone out.

DAD: She's not been out in two weeks.

ALICE: Mummy? Can you come and get me? I've got nothing left.

I don't know how to get home, mum. I've got nothing.

ALICE feels in her pockets and pulls out Jabberwocky.

I mean yeah, I've got this stupid *poem*, but –

She looks at the poem.

This is literally the last thing I've got.

Twas brillig and the – What, is this code, or an anagram, or –

Brillig. I mean what does brillig mean? I'm stuck on the second word. What's the point in even trying?

ALICE screws up the piece of paper and sits on the floor, her head in her hands.

A voice calls from the cupboard.

HUMPTY DUMPTY: Hey you! You at the back!

ALICE: What?

ALICE looks up, hastily wiping her eyes and stuffing the piece of paper back into her pocket.

HUMPTY DUMPTY appears out of the cupboard, sitting at a very high school desk.

HUMPTY DUMPTY: What are you doing there?

ALICE: Me? Nothing. I'm not doing anything.

ALICE stands up and turns to face him.

HUMPTY DUMPTY: That's hardly true, is it? You're standing, aren't you? You're looking. You're *breathing.* I'd say you were doing rather a lot.

ALICE doesn't say anything.

Don't answer back! It's your own time you're wasting, you know.

How old did you say you were?

ALICE: I'm twelve.

HUMPTY DUMPTY: Wrong! You never said anything of the sort.

ALICE: What?

HUMPTY DUMPTY: Try to stay awake.

ALICE: I thought you meant 'how old are you'?

HUMPTY DUMPTY: If I'd meant that, I'd have said it, wouldn't I?

Twelve, you say.

ALICE: Twelve and three weeks.

HUMPTY DUMPTY: An uncomfortable sort of age. If you'd asked my advice, I'd have said 'leave off at eleven', but it's too late now.

ALICE: What d'you mean, 'leave off'?

HUMPTY DUMPTY: Put up your hand if you want to say something.

ALICE puts her hand up.

ALICE: What d'you mean, 'leave off'?

HUMPTY DUMPTY: Stop. Stop growing.

ALICE: You can't stop growing.

HUMPTY DUMPTY: '*One*' can't stop growing. Speak properly.

ALICE: OK, one can't stop growing.

HUMPTY DUMPTY: One can't, but two can. With proper assistance you might have left off at eleven.

ALICE turns away.

It's all a choice, you know. Young people today – you're all about feelings – oh dear poor me, I've got a terrible life I'm very upset. Try being stuck up here talking to reprobates like you, then you'd know what upset is!

ALICE: *(Under her breath.)* Get down then.

HUMPTY DUMPTY: I beg your pardon?

ALICE: Nothing.

HUMPTY DUMPTY: WHAT DID YOU SAY?

ALICE: I said if you don't like it, why don't you get down?

HUMPTY DUMPTY: If *you* don't like it, why don't you buck your ideas up? Hmm? What have you got to say to that, Little Miss Backchat?

ALICE: I don't know what you mean by 'buck your ideas up'.

HUMPTY DUMPTY: Flummery – pure flummery.

ALICE shakes her head, confused.

What?

ALICE: I don't know what 'flummery' is.

HUMPTY's voice rises to a shriek as he speaks.

HUMPTY DUMPTY: Flummery is that way you have of standing there with your nose in the air as if you thought the world owed you something, as if it was your particular entitlement to live a life free from suffering, and why can't things just be nice and why doesn't anyone come and rescue me when they know perfectly well I'm stuck here and can't get down!

ALICE: But that's a huge amount of things for one word to mean, that's too much.

HUMPTY DUMPTY: When I say a word it means exactly what I choose it to mean. I am very very good with words. There isn't a word in the world that I don't know the meaning of.

ALICE realises something.

ALICE: Oh. You're a *word person*!

She reaches into her pocket and pulls out Jabberwocky again.

So maybe you could interpret this –

HUMPTY DUMPTY: THE BELL IS FOR ME NOT FOR YOU!

ALICE: What bell?

HUMPTY DUMPTY: You – you're in detention. Stay behind.

ALICE: Um. Right, OK. OK, can I ask you about these words I don't understand –

HUMPTY switches into a much more understanding tone.

HUMPTY DUMPTY: Now, what's going on here, eh? You can talk to me, you know. I'm not an ogre.

ALICE: No, of course. Thank you. I wanted to ask you –

HUMPTY DUMPTY: Anything you'd like to tell me about? Someone bullying you?

It's OK to tell someone, you know – if you tell someone we can do something about it. Everything alright at home?

ALICE: What?

HUMPTY DUMPTY: I'm just wondering what's making you behave like this. What d'you think the King would say if he knew?

ALICE: The King?

HUMPTY DUMPTY: I'm very good friends with the King. Do you know he told me if I was ever in trouble he'd send all of his horses and all of his men?

ALICE: Oh. Right. I'm supposed to know who you are.

I mean gosh, lucky me – to be standing talking to the real Humpty Dumpty.

HUMPTY DUMPTY: Oh you knew who I was, did you, when you saw me?

ALICE: You're famous. I'm sorry, I didn't like to say at first. I was a bit shy. Not everybody gets to have a poem explained to them by the real –

HUMPTY DUMPTY: Yes, I can see it would be probably the most exciting thing that ever happened to you.

ALICE: The King must be very honoured to know someone as clever as you. I bet he comes and talks to you all the time.

HUMPTY DUMPTY: Um, yes, well. He's a very busy man.

But he did give me this.

He shows ALICE his special blackboard pointer.

He gave it to me for an unbirthday present.

ALICE: Um, what's an unbirthday present?

HUMPTY DUMPTY: An unbirthday present is a present given when it's not your birthday. Unbirthdays are much better than birthdays. Do you know why?

ALICE: Um, no.

HUMPTY DUMPTY: How many days are there in a year?

ALICE: Um. Three hundred and sixty five. And a quarter.

HUMPTY DUMPTY: And how many birthdays do you have in a year?

ALICE: One.

HUMPTY DUMPTY: So if you take one from three hundred and sixty five,

ALICE: And a quarter.

HUMPTY DUMPTY: Don't get clever. If you take one from three hundred and sixty five and a quarter, what do you get?

ALICE: Three hundred and sixty four. And a quarter.

HUMPTY frowns.

Shall I write it down and hand it in?

HUMPTY DUMPTY: You know, with the amount of paperwork I have to do it's a wonder I have time to teach anything at all.

ALICE: OK, can you tell me what this poem means?

She takes Jabberwocky from her pocket.

HUMPTY DUMPTY: Ah. Poetry. My special pigeon.

Read me the first verse.

ALICE: OK.

> *(Reads.)*
> 'Twas Brillig and the slithy toves
> Did gyre and gimble in the wabe:
> All mimsy were the borogoves,
> And the mome raths outgrabe…

HUMPTY DUMPTY: What words in particular are troubling you?

ALICE: Most of them. I don't know what brillig means.

HUMPTY DUMPTY: Brillig is four o'clock in the afternoon – when you begin broiling things for supper.

ALICE: OK. That doesn't make very much sense, but –

HUMPTY DUMPTY: Carry on.

ALICE: Slithy?

HUMPTY DUMPTY: *Slithy.* That means lithe and slimy. What we call a portmanteau word – two words in one, two meanings packed in the same suitcase.

ALICE: And what are toves?

HUMPTY DUMPTY: Toves are a little like badgers, something like lizards and quite a lot like corkscrews.

ALICE: OK, gyre and gimble.

HUMPTY DUMPTY: Gyre is to go round and round like a gyroscope, gimble is to make holes like a gimlet.

ALICE: That doesn't make sense.

HUMPTY DUMPTY: It's not a very good poem.

ALICE: Mimsy?

HUMPTY DUMPTY: Flimsy and miserable.

ALICE: Borogoves?

HUMPTY DUMPTY: Thin, shabby looking birds with feathers that stick out all round.

ALICE: Mome raths?

HUMPTY DUMPTY: Raaths! To rhyme with baaths! Speak properly.

ALICE: Where I come from we say bath.

HUMPTY DUMPTY: A rath is a sort of a pig.

ALICE: Oh, ok, I saw a pig earlier.

HUMPTY DUMPTY: Mome means from home – as in someone who'd lost their way.

ALICE: Oh, that's me! I've lost my way home.

HUMPTY DUMPTY: One can only go so far with a conservative structure like that. Most poets of any worth these days have abandoned the rhyme entirely. We like to let our words roam free.

ALICE: Yes, so the next bit says –

HUMPTY DUMPTY: I said, WE like to let our words roam free.

ALICE: Right. You're a poet, are you?

HUMPTY DUMPTY: Oh no, I couldn't possibly.

ALICE: Sorry?

HUMPTY DUMPTY: It's so exposing to read one's work aloud – it's a very delicate process.

ALICE: OK, we could just carry on / with this then –

HUMPTY DUMPTY: Well, if you insist.

HUMPTY takes a piece of paper from his breast pocket.

ALICE: No, I don't insist, really.

HUMPTY DUMPTY: I can't bear to disappoint people, you see. But I'm still tinkering with this one, so –

ALICE: OK.

HUMPTY DUMPTY: It is called 'Sleeping With The Fishes'.

HUMPTY clears his throat.

Ahem.

I have slept with the fishes
Oh I oh I
Down in the murkiest depths
On a dark dark dark dark dark dark dark dark dark
Night

Repetition there, I don't know if you spotted it.

ALICE: Just about.

HUMPTY DUMPTY:

Sing us a story! Oh! Cry the fishes
For we are so scared that the spectre will come.

Up on the beach, the beach that is breadcrumbs
The prawns are a-dancing
And laugh with the waves

Anthropomorphism there, of course, since we know that
waves don't laugh.

ALICE: Neither do prawns.

HUMPTY DUMPTY:

Then out of the shadows, a-shuffling, a-groaning
Shuffling, stumpy
Slow and moaning

Assonance. Slow and moaning.

I'll sing you a song! Says the terrible spectre
Of earths that have worms in and things that eat eyes
The life underground is not fit to keep rats in
I AM NOT AT PEACE! the spectre cries

The rat, of course, a classical symbol for survival of the
human spirit.

Did you catch the reference to Finnegans Wake back
there?

ALICE: Absolutely. Just I've really got to –

HUMPTY DUMPTY:

Take thou my hand, and the hands of the fishes
Come with me dancing to infinite death
Oh oh oh oh
Do not let them burn me he cries

ALICE: Thank you, I've really got to –

HUMPTY DUMPTY: I haven't finished.

Nails clawing at the lid of the coffin

ALICE: I think I've had enough poetry now.

HUMPTY DUMPTY:

I AM NOT AT PEACE! he cries
DO NOT BURN ME, I AM NOT AT PEACE!

ALICE: Stop it!

HUMPTY DUMPTY:

Deep. Deep. Deep. Deep.
Sleeping with the fishes
I AM NOT AT PEACE.

ALICE: Stop it now! I mean it.

ALICE shakes a little.

HUMPTY DUMPTY: I have never been spoken to like that.

ALICE: Sorry. Sorry, just –

HUMPTY DUMPTY: You can interpret your own poem, and good luck to you, I say.

ALICE: No I'm sorry. Please can you –

HUMPTY DUMPTY: THE BELL IS FOR ME NOT FOR YOU!

Homework in by Friday please, or there'll be no jam for anyone. It's your own life you're wasting, you know…

Some WONDERLANDERS come and wheel HUMPTY off.

ALICE: Yeah, well done, Alice, that's excellent. He could have explained that whole thing to you, but now you've pissed him off and he's pissed off, gone away. Fat lot of good you turned out to be.

ALICE sees the POSTMAN approaching. She pulls herself together.

OH, OK. Here we go. Hello.

The POSTMAN doesn't seem to see her.

Hello?

POSTMAN: Hello?

ALICE: Hi.

The POSTMAN smiles blandly and carries on.

Haven't you got anything for me? In there?

The POSTMAN stops, looks at ALICE.

POSTMAN: Don't think so.

ALICE: Um, sorry, could you – would you mind checking?

Please.

He opens the post box and starts to go through it.

POSTMAN: I do have a round to do, you know.

ALICE: Yes, thank you.

POSTMAN: What's the name?

ALICE: Alice. You gave me a letter before.

POSTMAN: Not ringing any bells, I'm afraid.

He pulls out a bucket and spade and hands it to ALICE.

This any good to you?

ALICE: Um, not really.

POSTMAN: How about this?

He pulls out a pair of flip flops tied together.

ALICE: No, I was thinking more like a –

POSTMAN: What about this – lovely.

He pulls out an ice cream and holds it towards ALICE.

ALICE: For god's sake I don't want stupid knick-knacks I want something *proper*. What am I going to do with a bloody bucket and spade? I need a letter or a postcard or I don't know, a message written on a piece of *bark* I mean something useful that'll tell me what to do cause I don't know what to do.

POSTMAN: Well.

ALICE: Sorry.

POSTMAN: Just trying to do my job.

ALICE: I'm sorry.

POSTMAN: Under trying circumstances.

ALICE: I just want to go home. I saw you and I thought you must be coming to give me something.

ALICE looks away. The POSTMAN softens.

POSTMAN: Let's have another look, shall we?

He starts to go through the box again. He pulls out a plastic cricket bat, but thinks better of giving it to ALICE, and puts it back in.

POSTMAN: Can't see anything for an Alice, I'm afraid. What's the surname?

ALICE: Little.

POSTMAN: Little. Nope.

The POSTMAN pulls out a plastic wrapped skate shop catalogue.

Got a Joseph Little, I'm guessing that's not you.

ALICE: Joe.

The POSTMAN hands the catalogue to ALICE.

He gets these all the time, this is the only kind of post he gets, this and guitar catalogues. We'll have to cancel them.

POSTMAN: Sorry, d'you know this person?

ALICE: Yeah.

POSTMAN: Don't fancy delivering that for me, do you?

ALICE hands the catalogue back.

ALICE: He's not here.

POSTMAN: Ah well. Pop it back in. Never know when you might bump into someone.

ALICE: No, I mean he's gone.

POSTMAN: Gone's where I should be. These knick-knacks won't deliver themselves, you know.

ALICE: *(To herself.)* He's gone.

POSTMAN: Cheerio then.

The POSTMAN leaves.

ALICE: Gone for always. I'll never get to tell him I –

We'll never have popcorn together and watch a dvd again. He'll never do that funny face behind mum's back when she's being – We'll never go for a bike ride. He won't be there to take me to the pub when I'm big enough. I was dreading him going to university next year but he won't even be going to university now.

The *stupid* – Why was he so stupid? He knows how to cross the road. He bloody taught *me* how to cross the road.

ALICE hears a strain of the birthday song Joe wrote for her.

Joe?

She listens for a moment, then the song fades away.

No no, don't go – I can't remember the words. Joe?

Don't cry – Don't cry, Alice, don't –

She's interrupted by a crying wail somewhere close by. She turns around, looking for where the sound came from.

Two voices are heard approaching.

MOCK TURTLE: Oh no. This is a disaster.

GRYPHON: Now love, let me just – I just need to get hold of your hands and we'll try to flip you, OK. We'll get you upright in no time.

Hup hup *heave!*

The GRYPHON and MOCK TURTLE appear – she's flat on her back (as much as you can be with a tin bath strapped to your back) and he is pulling on her hands to try to flip her over, but only succeeds in pulling her along the floor, closer to ALICE.

MOCK TURTLE: It's no good, you'll never get me't right way up again. I'll have to spend't rest of my life flat on my back.

GRYPHON: Might be quite nice.

MOCK TURTLE: And since I've got this terrible cold,

GRYPHON: You haven't got a cold love, it's just nerves.

MOCK TURTLE: I know what'll happen – the snot'll all go backwards down my throat and I'll choke to death and I'll be powerless to stop it, and won't they all laugh at me. Choking to death.

GRYPHON: There's someone over there. They might be able to help.

The MOCK TURTLE cranes her head to look.

MOCK TURTLE: It won't work. We'll just be disappointed.

The GRYPHON comes over to ALICE.

GRYPHON: Hello.

ALICE: Hi.

GRYPHON: Don't suppose you'd give us a hand, would you?

ALICE: OK.

GRYPHON: Thank you. Thanks everso much.

The GRYPHON and ALICE walk over to the MOCK TURTLE.

Thing is my wife's got a bit –

MOCK TURTLE: Hello.

GRYPHON: Got a bit upset.

MOCK TURTLE: I'm *very* upset.

GRYPHON: Upset in the sense of being overturned.

MOCK TURTLE: Disturbed!

GRYPHON: I think it might take two of us to get her back again.

ALICE: OK, why don't you pull that foot over?

GRYPHON: Yes.

ALICE: And I'll pull this hand – sorry, can I have your hand? Other one.

The MOCK TURTLE grudgingly gives ALICE her hand.

MOCK TURTLE: It's never going to work.

I mean whose idea was it to go for a walk, anyway?

ALICE: OK, and then if we both pull at the same time…

GRYPHON: It was a lovely walk – we went all along't beach.

MOCK TURTLE: Sand made my toes itch.

ALICE: Pull a bit harder!

GRYPHON: We had a paddle, talked about old times. It were lovely.

MOCK TURTLE: It were *terrible.*

ALICE: Once more!

They finally pull hard enough and the MOCK TURTLE flips over onto her hands and knees.

MOCK TURTLE: Ooof.

ALICE: There we go.

Can I help you stand up?

GRYPHON: One hand each.

They each take one of the MOCK TURTLE's hands and help her to stand up.

Well int it nice to be't right way up again?

The MOCK TURTLE won't let go of ALICE's hand.

MOCK TURTLE: No – lead me to't sofa, I'm too weak to stand.

ALICE: Sofa?

GRYPHON: Over there.

ALICE looks over and sees a battered sofa sitting on the beach.

ALICE: A sofa on a beach. I'm not even surprised anymore.

MOCK TURTLE: I mean this is why I prefer not to go for walks and things – 'cause when I fall over I can't get back up again.

It is so terribly hard on me.

The MOCK TURTLE starts to wail. Then, after a moment –

Tissue!

The GRYPHON grabs a box of tissues and hands one to the MOCK TURTLE.

It's my husband I feel sorry for, really.

GRYPHON: No, love.

MOCK TURTLE: What can it be like, being stuck wi' me all't time?

The MOCK TURTLE blows her nose loudly on the tissue, then puts her hand out for another.

I have been *so* ill for so long.

ALICE: What's wrong with you?

GRYPHON: What's not wrong with her?

MOCK TURTLE: You see? The burden I am?

I used to be a dancer, you know. I wish you could have seen. I can hardly move now for't terrible pain in my back

– rheumatic, phlegmatic, asthmatic, operatic, you name it I've got it.

Tissue!

The GRYPHON reaches into the tissues box, but it's empty.

GRYPHON: They're all gone, love.

MOCK TURTLE: Oh no!

ALICE: What?

MOCK TURTLE: All't tissues have gone. This is aaaaaawful. This is a disaster.

ALICE: It's not really a –

MOCK TURTLE: How is this not a disaster? How can I wipe my eyes if there aren't any more tissues?

GRYPHON: No no, tell her about the dancing, love.

ALICE: It's OK, you don't have to –

GRYPHON: D'you want her to stop crying? Go on love – the night we met.

MOCK TURTLE: All-Wonderland Maritime Dance Championship. Right here on this very beach.

GRYPHON: Bit smarter then.

MOCK TURTLE: There were strings of twinkling lights.

GRYPHON: I saw the Mock Turtle from across a crowded dance floor.

MOCK TURTLE: The Cuttlefish Rumba!

GRYPHON: Just something in the turn of her wrist, the extension of her arm, and that were it, that were me – gone!

ALICE: And did you see him, too?

MOCK TURTLE: He danced as if he had wings.

GRYPHON: I was thinner back then.

MOCK TURTLE: All I wanted was for him to come and introduce himself.

GRYPHON: I waited for the Anchovy Quickstep.

MOCK TURTLE: And that were it, that were me – gone!

GRYPHON: We've hardly been apart since.

MOCK TURTLE: Quickstepping all over Wonderland. But it's all gone now!

GRYPHON: No love, no no no – remember our song?

MOCK TURTLE: Of course I do.

GRYPHON: Why don't you sing it for her?

ALICE: No, it's OK, I'm sure I can just imagine –

MOCK TURTLE: If she doesn't want to hear it –

The GRYPHON raises his eyebrows at ALICE.

ALICE: No, please. I'd love to.

GRYPHON: There you go love.

Just after we danced together for the first time, we were sitting over a delicious bowl of pea soup, the fairy lights all twinkling – and she started, ever so softly, to sing:

MOCK TURTLE: *(Sings.)*
Beautiful Soup, so rich and green,
Waiting in a hot tureen!
Who for such dainties would not stoop?
Soup of the evening, beautiful Soup!
Soup of the evening, beautiful Soup!

ALICE: It's a song about soup.

GRYPHON: She sang it at our wedding, too.

MOCK TURTLE:
Beau-ootiful Soo-oop!
Beau-ootiful Soo-oop!
Soo-oop of the e-e-evening,
Beautiful, beautiful Soup!

By the end of the song, the MOCK TURTLE is standing up.

GRYPHON: Beautiful, my love. Int it?

ALICE: It's the best song about soup I've ever heard.

The MOCK TURTLE sits down again.

MOCK TURTLE: It were a long time ago.

GRYPHON: We were champions, weren't we, love?

MOCK TURTLE: Till I lost it.

The GRYPHON goes behind the sofa and pulls out a number of trophies which he hands to the MOCK TURTLE, who hands them to ALICE.

GRYPHON: Tuna Samba, Salmon Cha Cha Cha.

ALICE: Lost what?

MOCK TURTLE: My confidence. Left it in a dressing room once, came back couldn't find it anywhere and that was the end of it all.

GRYPHON: That's when she took to wearing that thing.

Look love, Lobster Quadrille…

ALICE: What's a Lobster Quadrille?

GRYPHON: The Lobster Quadrille is a stately and beautiful dance.

MOCK TURTLE: It is very beautiful. I shall never dance it again.

ALICE: How d'you know?

MOCK TURTLE: I'm in constant pain. My back.

ALICE: Is that maybe because you've got a tin bath strapped to you?

MOCK TURTLE: Sorry?

ALICE: Well that's got to be heavy, hasn't it? Maybe that's what's making your back hurt.

MOCK TURTLE: What does she mean?

ALICE: I mean why have you got a big tin bath strapped to you?

MOCK TURTLE: I need it for support.

ALICE: It's not much support if it's making you fall over all the time.

MOCK TURTLE: I'm very delicate – I need protecting.

ALICE: From what?

MOCK TURTLE: World's full of sharp things and germs and things that want to hurt you –

The MOCK TURTLE looks at the GRYPHON.

This is making me very upset.

ALICE: I mean what if it's *you* that's holding you back – what if it's just that funny fake shell you're wearing? You might find your confidence again if you took that thing off.

GRYPHON: Now it's not her fault she's –

ALICE: Why d'you let her get away with it? What if she could have been dancing all this time? All this time you've wasted feeling sorry for yourselves.

The GRYPHON stops, nods.

MOCK TURTLE: Why aren't you looking after me?

GRYPHON: You know, she might have a point, love.

ALICE: Maybe getting a bit of exercise would make you feel better.

GRYPHON: Bit of fresh air through your lungs.

MOCK TURTLE: My poor lungs!

The GRYPHON comes close to the MOCK TURTLE.

GRYPHON: Wouldn't being able to dance again be nicer than anything? Nicer even than being poorly and being looked after? Remember what it used to feel like?

Why don't we try taking't shell off, eh? See how it feels.

MOCK TURTLE: But what if I take it off and something bad happens?

GRYPHON: If we're together, it doesn't matter if something bad happens.

This girl needs us to teach her the Lobster Quadrille –

ALICE: Oh god do I have to dance?

GRYPHON: *(To Alice.)* Please?

ALICE: Yeah, OK.

GRYPHON: You see? Are we going to let her learn it off someone substandard?

MOCK TURTLE: No, you're right, love.

GRYPHON: Can I unstrap it, then?

MOCK TURTLE: Yes. Gently.

The GRYPHON looks to ALICE for help, and together they undo the straps tying the bath to the MOCK TURTLE's back.

GRYPHON: Just this last one… There.

ALICE: Can you stand up?

They help her stand up, but she nearly overbalances.

MOCK TURTLE: Aaahh –

GRYPHON: Hold on to me.

She regains her balance.

MOCK TURTLE: Yes. Yes. There we are.

GRYPHON: *(To Alice.)* Now the Lobster Quadrille starts like this –

The MOCK TURTLE suddenly wails.

MOCK TURTLE: No no no, wait wait –

GRYPHON: Oh my love, come on –

MOCK TURTLE: No, I mean. I'm not properly dressed.

The MOCK TURTLE takes off her grubby housecoat to reveal a fabulous ballgown underneath.

ALICE: Wow.

MOCK TURTLE: Now I'm ready.

GRYPHON: Don't you look a picture?

(To Alice.) Now take my hand and I'll take the Mock Turtle's hand and we go like this – step, step-step

Good, and again – step, step-step

MOCK TURTLE: Fingers, darling. Think lobster.

The MOCK TURTLE demonstrates a hand position vaguely reminiscent of a lobster claw.

GRYPHON: Step, step-step. Step, step-step. And then the words go –

"Will you walk a little faster?" said a whiting to a snail,
"There's a porpoise close behind us, and he's treading on my tail.
See how eagerly the lobsters and the turtles all advance!
They are waiting on the shingle – will you come and join the dance?
Will you, won't you, will you, won't you, will you join the dance?
Will you, won't you, will you, won't you, won't you join the dance?

MOCK TURTLE: Got the hang of it?

ALICE: I think so.

GRYPHON: And faster for the second verse:

"You can really have no notion how delightful it will be
When they take us up and throw us, with the lobsters, out to sea!"
But the snail replied "Too far, too far!" and gave a look askance –
Said he thanked the whiting kindly but he would not join the dance.

Will you, won't you, will you, won't you, will you join the
dance?
Will you, won't you, will you, won't you, won't you join
the dance?

MOCK TURTLE: And then all the lobsters join in!

*The beach is filled with dancing lobsters. The GRYPHON and MOCK
TURTLE lead the dance expertly, enthused by each others' talent.*

The dance gets faster and faster and ALICE struggles to keep up.

*As the dance ends, ALICE tries to get her breath back. She laughs as
the MOCK TURTLE and GRYPHON dance away from her, followed
by the lobsters.*

ALICE marks through the steps she's learned, dancing on her own.

ALICE: And one two three LOBSTER one two three PRAWN
one two three CUTTLEFISH

Strictly Come Lobster. Brilliant. One two three PRAWN.

No, that's not right – one two three PRAWN gosh it's
difficult.

She stops, thinking. Realises something.

Completely inappropriate. COMPLETELY inappropriate.

God, if my mum saw me dancing. That is totally. That is
not OK. What, Joe's dead and I'm dancing around? Idiot.
God, Alice, what were you thinking?

*She hears a noise approaching – the shouts of excited small children
– and looks to see where the sound is coming from.*

*Two boys in prep school uniform (shorts, blazers and peaked caps)
cycle in on small tricycles. One has a tiny guitar strapped to his
back, the other an accordion. They're shouting their own version of
'Cock-a-doodle-doo'.*

DUM/DEE: Tweedle-eedle-

DUM: DUM!

DUM/DEE: Tweedle-eedle-

DEE: DEE!

DUM/DEE: Tweedle-eedle-…

They both stop and look around them as if they've lost something.

Then they see ALICE.

DUM: Look! A lady!

They cycle towards her and start going round her in circles.

DEE: Look how fast I can go!

DUM: Look how fast I can go!

DEE: I can do a clap while I'm going, look –

He lifts his hands from the handlebars and claps, then puts them back very quickly.

DUM: And we can do this, look –

They cycle towards each other, doing a high 5 as they pass each other.

BOTH: Woo-hoo!

DEE: And I can do a wheelie – I'm going to do one now.

He cycles to a corner, pointing diagonally towards ALICE.

Watch, right, watch.

He cycles towards her, then lifts the front wheel of his tricycle about 3 inches off the ground.

Woo! Look, woo!

DUM: 'Mazin.

DEE stops and looks at ALICE.

DEE: Clap then!

ALICE claps.

ALICE: Yes, very good, well done.

They get off their tricycles (with a big movement, as if dismounting from a Harley Davidson) and high 5 each other again, then turn their attention back to ALICE.

DUM: Watch this, right – I'm going to do my dance. Watch my dance.

DUM does a sort-of hip-hop dance.

Check this out, right.

DEE: Them is some killer moves!

Don't laugh at him.

ALICE: I'm not.

DUM: And then I go like this –

And then it finishes like this.

And then you clap.

ALICE: Brilliant.

ALICE claps. The boys high 5 each other.

DEE: Let's show her the other one.

DUM: Is she ready for it, though?

DEE: D'you want to see the coolest thing you've ever seen?

DUM: I don't think she could handle it.

ALICE: I probably could.

DEE: OK, but don't have a seizure or anything.

ALICE: I won't.

DUM: You might.

DEE: Ladies and Gentlemen: the Human Pyramid!

They go down on their hands and knees next to each other.

DUM: Ta dah!

DEE: Clap then.

ALICE: That's a pyramid, is it?

DUM: What?

DEE: Course it's a pyramid.

ALICE: It's just you two kneeling down next to each other. Shouldn't there be another person on the top?

The boys look at each other, realising.

DUM: Oh.

DEE: Oh yeah.

DUM: Doesn't do without Doo, does it?

DEE: No can Doo.

ALICE: Pardon?

DUM: Tweedledoo goes on the top.

ALICE: Tweedle –

DUM: Doo.

ALICE: Sorry, what?

The boys sigh at having to explain.

DEE: He's Tweedledum.

DUM: He's Tweedledee.

DEE: And our friend is called Tweedle*doo*.

DUM: Except we don't know where he's gone to.

DEE: He was here and then he's gone away.

ALICE: Did he say where he was going?

DEE: He didn't say anything.

DUM: One day he was there and the next day he wasn't.

DEE: And we was a bit sad.

DUM: And now there's only two of us, which means we can't do a proper pyramid AND we can't be a proper band.

ALICE: A music band?

DEE: He plays ukulele and I play ukulele and then Tweedledoo is the main guitar man.

DUM: And the singer.

DEE: And he writes the songs.

DUM: And you can't be a band with only two.

ALICE: What was the band called?

DEE: The Doodeedums.

DUM: Which is a name made out of –

ALICE: Your names, yeah.

DEE: She's clever, she is.

DUM: Swotty, she's a swot.

ALICE: Why can't you be in a band with only two?

DEE: Can't even decide what we're called. I think The Deedums.

DUM: I think the Dumdees.

DEE: But that's a stupid name.

DUM: Yeah, bum off, poo man.

DEE: Poo off, bum man.

DUM: You're a man made out of poo.

DEE: You're a man made out of bums.

ALICE: Boys, come on –

DEE: He pretends to be my friend, you know, but he STOLE my maraca.

DUM: I DID NOT STEAL YOUR MARACA.

DEE: He stole it and it was a new one.

DUM: It's my job to do the maraca bit in the middle of the song.

DEE: But it's my maraca, so you can't. He's a stealer.

DUM: It's not your maraca, it's ours.

ALICE: Why don't you just share it, OK? How's that?

DEE: Fight you for it!

ALICE: Share it.

DUM: OK, fight for it, then. Good luck cause you're going to need it.

DEE: You are too, cause I'm the best fighter.

The boys square up, fists raised.

ALICE: OK, OK, hang on –

DEE: Think you can fight me without armour?

DUM: Think you can?

DEE: Ding ding ding that's the bell to get tooled up.

The boys lower their fists.

DUM: She can help us get ready.

They toddle off and each return pulling an old-fashioned trunk containing makeshift armour – pillows, saucepans, hubcaps, a colander, a couple of muffin trays and a tangle of rope and string.

They start to get dressed, tying the metal objects and the pillows to themselves.

DEE: Can you tie this round the back, please?

ALICE goes to help him.

TWEEDLEDUM puts a saucepan on his head.

DUM: Helmet on –

TWEEDLEDEE points to the colander.

DEE: I need that for my head.

ALICE picks it up for him.

It's got holes in cause it's breathable, see?

DUM: Gonna hurt you big, bum man.

DEE: *(Quietly.)* Maybe I shouldn't fight today, you know, cause I've actually got asthma.

DUM: I need help too!

ALICE: Coming.

ALICE goes to help TWEEDLEDUM tie a muffin tray to his front.

DUM: I'm going to need a weapon.

DEE: You're a weapon.

DUM: *You're* a weapon.

DEE: I'm taking you to Painful Town, population *you.*

DUM: *(To ALICE.)* Maybe I shouldn't fight today, you know, cause I've got a bone in my leg.

ALICE: You don't have to fight.

DUM: He'll think I'm a baby if I don't.

DEE: I don't want to fight today, I'm too sad.

DUM: I'm too sad too.

We didn't have fighting when Tweedledoo was here.

DEE: We did a bit.

DUM: But Tweedledoo would stop us fighting, or he'd do something funny so we wouldn't want to.

ALICE: My brother used to say 'don't laugh don't laugh don't laugh' till I couldn't stop myself laughing.

DUM: Has your brother gone away too?

ALICE: Yeah. Never coming back.

The three of them sit down on one of the trunks, dejected.

DEE: It hurts here.

DUM: Yeah.

ALICE: That's where your heart is.

DUM: And my tummy.

ALICE: Oh. I was looking for something to do with a Heart, wasn't I?

DUM: Also my arms and legs hurt.

DEE: My hands are all heavy and sad.

ALICE: So are mine.

DUM: You know what Tweedledoo can do?

ALICE: No, what?

DUM: He can go along on his bike and play his guitar at the same time.

DEE: I can do that.

DUM: No you can't.

ALICE: Boys –

DUM: Do you remember when Tweedledoo did a massive fart and we all ran away and left it for someone to find?

DEE: That was so funny, man.

Do you remember when we tried to teach him burping and he couldn't even do it?

DUM: That was awesome.

DEE: *(Burps.)* Like that and he couldn't even do it.

DUM: I laughed so much my hat came off.

DEE: I laughed so much my shoes came off.

DUM: I laughed so much my pants came off.

Not really. It was well funny, though.

ALICE: How can you talk about it?

DUM: What?

ALICE: Happy things. Remembering happy things.

DUM: What d'you mean?

ALICE: When I think about my brother it makes me feel sick so I mostly try and think about something else.

DEE: But you've got to remember the happy things. When I think about happy times it makes it like he's still here a little bit.

DUM: It stops me being so sad.

DEE: Specially if I think about doing our songs with Doo when we was in our band.

Shall we show the lady?

DUM: But Doo's not here.

DEE: D'you know the words?

DUM: A bit. Do you?

DEE: Sort of.

DUM: Come on then.

They get ready to play.

But don't clap till the end, alright?

ALICE: OK.

DUM: Ladies and ladies – the Dumdees!

DEE: The Deedums!

DUM: A 1-2-3-4…

TWEEDLEDUM and TWEEDLEDEE play their song, though struggle to remember the words:

DUM/DEE: *(Singing.)*
There was a walrus
He went a walking
He was all tusky and all husky and all grey

There was a carpenter
He was mates with the walrus
They went a-walking on the beach one lovely day

Can you remember the next bit?
There's a bit about oysters
Something else before that duh duh duh duh duh

Now it's the oysters
They eat the oysters
(spoken:) Oh you divv, that's the end what are you doing?

They asked the oysters
To come a-walking
They made them walk quite fast because they were quite
fat

They had some bread with them
They had some vinegar
Oysters didn't see what's funny about that

La la la walking
La la la oysters
They didn't even try to run away

Is this the bit where
They all get eaten?
For the oysters it was not a happy day

You stupid oysters
To trust a walrus
To trust a carpenter with vinegar and bread

Cause they got eaten
Yeah they got eaten UP!
And after that the oysters were all dead

(Slow right down for this – like a cadenza:.)
It was a lovely night
Down on the beach that day
Who would have thought it would have ended that way…

(all on one note:.)
What do we do now?
Go back to the beginning.

(Go back to the start and repeat…)

A courtroom has formed around ALICE and the TWEEDLES. A throne-like chair in the centre, with a witness box to one side.

On the other side twelve chairs are arranged, and a jury of WONDERLANDERS (with a few lobsters mixed in.) are taking their seats.

On a small occasional table a cake stand is covered with a black cloth.

A Court OFFICIAL approaches to stop the TWEEDLES' song.

OFFICIAL: Come along now, pack it in – no music in court, please.

DUM: Yeah alright alright we were going to stop anyway.

ALICE: In *court?*

OFFICIAL: Quiet in court!

The WHITE RABBIT is also there.

WHITE RABBIT: All rise for the King and Queen!

Everyone stands up.

The KING and QUEEN process into the courtroom. The QUEEN takes her place on the throne, the KING sits at a desk to the side.

Everyone follows the WHITE RABBIT's instructions:

Raise your right hand.

Make a W.

Make an L.

Do a fish.

Please be seated.

Everyone sits down.

Your majesty.

QUEEN: Me are here today to sit in judgement upon a grave and dismaying matter. A disgraceful crime that must be investigated – and punished – in the biggest and most public way possible. By me.

JURY MEMBER: String him up!

QUEEN: Off with his head! Would I settle the matter out of court, they said, save myself the upset? But I said to them, as I say to you: no way. No settling. Me believe we owe it – we owe it to *jam* to see justice done, no matter how painful the –

The queen is almost overcome with emotion, but recovers herself.

KING: Shall we continue this later, my dear?

QUEEN: Bring in the criminal!

KING: The *defendant.*

WHITE RABBIT: Bring in the defendant!

To booing and hissing from the public gallery the KNAVE is brought in – handcuffed – and once he is in place, is cordoned off so that he's standing in a small square pen.

ALICE: It's him – it *was* him, I saw it. I'm a witness.

I'm right at the heart of the action. Right at the Heart. This must be the final level, this must be the thing before I get to go home, mustn't it?

QUEEN: Read the accusation.

The WHITE RABBIT stands and reads the following:

WHITE RABBIT: The queen of Hearts, she made some tarts,
All on a summer's day:
The Knave of Hearts, he stole those tarts
And took them quite away.

QUEEN: The rotter! Jury – consider your verdict.

WHITE RABBIT: Your majesty, there's a lot to happen before that.

KING: The Knave of Hearts –

QUEEN: Or "Johnny Tart Thief".

KNAVE: Objection!

QUEEN: Overspent!

Show the evidence!

The WHITE RABBIT whisks away the black cloth, to show a plate of tarts.

WHITE RABBIT: The tarts, your majesty, which were retrieved from the Knave of Hearts' knapsack.

KNAVE: Untrue! Someone must have put them there.

QUEEN: Cover them over. My beautiful tarts.

The WHITE RABBIT replaces the cloth over the tarts.

WHITE RABBIT: Ladies and gentlemen of the jury, let us now consider the evidence. Appearing for the crown, his majesty the King.

QUEEN: All rise!

Everyone starts to stand up.

KING: No no, my dear, not now.

Unsure what to do, everyone shufflingly sits down again.

Call the first witness!

WHITE RABBIT: Call Mr M. Hatter!

The call is heard being repeated down the hallway several times, then the HATTER's voice is heard approaching.

HATTER: *(Off.)* Yes yes, I'm coming I'm coming. Get your hands off me. Can't a chap finish his tea first?

The HATTER flies into court, as if pushed backwards. He has a cup of tea in one hand, and a piece of bread and butter in the other.

When he sees the QUEEN he bows low.

Your majesty.

QUEEN: I know you.

HATTER: Yes, your majesty. I was, lately, milliner to the queen.

KING: Mr Hatter – I understand you saw the tarts being stolen by the Knave.

KNAVE: Objection! Leading the witness.

QUEEN: Overegged.

KING: Mr Hatter?

HATTER: Yes yes, I saw it. I saw him take the tarts.

KING: Go on – where were you?

HATTER: I was standing on the edge of the woods, just minding my own business when I saw the royal tarts being taken for a cooling stroll and I thought aw bless her, bless the queen –

QUEEN: Get on with it.

HATTER: Yes, so just as I was thinking this, along comes a man and takes the tarts clean away. Horrified, I was. Rooted to the spot.

KING: Did you have a good look at the man?

HATTER: I've never seen a more evil looking face.

KING: And do you see the man here in court?

HATTER: Yes, your majesty. Him.

The HATTER points at the WHITE RABBIT. The public gallery gasps.

The QUEEN coughs.

I mean him, there.

The HATTER points at the KNAVE.

The Knave of Hearts. Definitely him.

KING: No further questions.

The KING sits down at his desk.

WHITE RABBIT: Appearing for the defence: The Knave of Hearts.

ALICE: He's defending himself?

KNAVE: Mr Hatter –

The KNAVE looks at the KING, pointing to the barrier around him.

I can't – I can't do it from behind here, can I?

QUEEN: Then you shouldn't have stolen the tarts!

KNAVE: Can I come out for the cross-examination at least?

KING: Let him out. But keep an eye on him.

One side of the pen is opened by an OFFICIAL, and the KNAVE comes out.

KNAVE: Mr Hatter?

HATTER: Yes.

KNAVE: Mr M. Hatter.

HATTER: Yes.

KNAVE: What does the M stand for?

HATTER: I don't know, um. Nothing.

KNAVE: Do you like jam, Mr Hatter?

HATTER: Oh yes. Who doesn't like jam?

KNAVE: How often would you say you got to enjoy some lovely jam?

HATTER: Oh, hardly ever. All jam property of the queen.

KNAVE: What if there was some jam the queen didn't know about?

HATTER: I don't know what jam you mean.

The KNAVE is standing close to the HATTER and changes his tone, switching to a friendlier voice.

KNAVE: Mr Hatter, you said you were just having your tea?

HATTER: Oh yes. Tea time.

KNAVE: What would you normally have for your tea? On a normal day?

HATTER: Tea.

KNAVE: And to eat?

HATTER: Bread and butter.

KNAVE: That's a nice necktie, by the way.

HATTER: Thank you very much.

KNAVE: Shame it's got something on it.

The HATTER looks down at the tie.

HATTER: Oh, just a bit of jam.

The courtroom gasps in horror. The HATTER realises too late that he's been tricked.

I mean – I mean –

That? Oh, just a bit of Hendersons.

The KNAVE turns to the court OFFICIAL who has been furiously writing down everything being said.

KNAVE: Would you read back what the Hatter said to me in response to my question about the spot on his necktie?

OFFICIAL: 'Oh just a bit of jam'

KNAVE: '*Oh just a bit of jam*'. Ladies and Gentlemen of the jury, I would ask you to consider carefully the trustworthiness of this man's evidence. I would say that Mr M Hatter – what does the M stand for again?

HATTER: Mad.

KNAVE: Mad?

HATTER: But it doesn't mean –

KNAVE: How can we take anything this man says seriously when he's both mad and a jam smuggler?

HATTER: I haven't done anything.

KNAVE: Where did you get the jam from, then? *The inside of a tart?*

The HATTER points at the QUEEN.

HATTER: She gave it to me! They brought it on a teaspoon. They said 'pretend you saw it and you'll get a whole jar'.

The courtroom gasps. The QUEEN blushes.

QUEEN: Oh well, everybody knows he did it anyway.

KING: Witness dismissed.

The HATTER is manhandled out of the court by several officials.

HATTER: I'm sorry your majesty! I'm sorry.

QUEEN: Off with his head!

The QUEEN settles back into her chair, unable to look the KING in the eye.

KING: Next witness?

The KNAVE is led back to the pen, and the square is closed around him.

WHITE RABBIT: Call the Duchess!

The call echoes down the hall again.

KING: I hope you haven't messed with this one, my dear.

The DUCHESS is brought in and curtsies elaborately to the QUEEN.

DUCHESS: Dearest Queenie.

The QUEEN folds her arms and looks away.

QUEEN: Can't stand the sight of her.

DUCHESS: Now don't be a meanie Queenie – I've come to help you.

The DUCHESS tries to get closer to the QUEEN but a couple of officials lead her to the witness box.

The KING stands up to question her.

KING: Just to confirm your identity, you are –

DUCHESS: I saw it. I saw it happen. I was standing at the edge of the wood, close to where I live, just minding my own business when out of nowhere, *he* comes along. Mr Sneaky.

The Knave of Hearts. And takes the tarts clean away. Ask the poor cook's boy, he was as shocked as I was.

QUEEN: The cook's boy is no longer with us.

DUCHESS: Dismissed?

QUEEN: His head was dismissed from his shoulders, yes.

DUCHESS: I could tell, you know, what wonderful tarts they were. Organic flour, locally sourced, seasonal ingredients –

QUEEN: Oh shut up. Get her off.

KING: Thank you, no further questions.

DUCHESS: Don't you want to ask me about –

KING: Your witness.

The KNAVE once again steps out from behind his barrier and approaches the witness box.

KNAVE: The Duchess and I already know each other, of course, having both enjoyed the Queen's best-friendship at one time. Happy days, yes?

DUCHESS: I was at the palace every day. We'd talk, go shopping…

KNAVE: And I suppose you imagined that would always be the case.

DUCHESS: Yes.

KNAVE: But then something happened, didn't it?

DUCHESS: A baby happened. And she stopped wanting to be friends with me.

QUEEN: A terrible child!

KNAVE: She seemed, suddenly, what – frosty? Dismissive?

DUCHESS: Angry – I didn't know what I'd done.

The KNAVE hands the DUCHESS a tissue.

KNAVE: So when you saw me stealing the tarts that must have seemed like a good opportunity – when you saw me pinching those delicious tarts – what flavour were they? I've forgotten.

DUCHESS: Apricot.

KNAVE: Apricot jam tarts.

DUCHESS: Yes.

KNAVE: When you saw me walking away with an armful of *apricot* jam tarts –

KING: Objection! Leading the witness.

The KNAVE pulls off the cloth covering the tarts.

Ladies and gentlemen of the jury, I think you'll agree with me that these tarts are without a shadow of a doubt made with strawberry rather than apricot jam.

DUCHESS: I'm colourblind!

KNAVE: I put it to you, Duchess, that you took it upon yourself to come here without the least evidence, purely for personal gain –

QUEEN: Witness dismissed.

DUCHESS: But I only wanted to please you –

QUEEN: Off with her head!

The DUCHESS is led out of the courtroom, wailing.

The officials try to lead the KNAVE back to his pen, but he struggles.

KNAVE You can't put me in there now – you haven't got a leg to stand on.

QUEEN: I've got as many legs to stand on as I want – I won't have it – *someone* must have seen what happened –

The QUEEN looks around the courtroom. ALICE stands and puts her hand up.

ALICE: I did.

The courtroom turns to look at ALICE.

That is, I um. I saw him take them.

The KING comes over to ALICE.

KING: Did you *really*?

ALICE: I really did, I promise.

The KING turns to the QUEEN.

KING: Permission to call another witness.

QUEEN: Bestowed!

The KNAVE comes towards ALICE, snarling, but is led back to his pen by the officials.

WHITE RABBIT: Call Alice!

ALICE is led to the witness box. The KING approaches.

KING: Now, tell the court what you saw, as much as you can remember.

Take your time.

ALICE: I was standing near where the Hatter lives,

KING: Minding your own business?

ALICE: I was trying to work out how to get home. And I saw a boy pulling a trolley with some tarts on it. And then when the boy wasn't looking I saw the Knave –

KING: Did you know who he was?

ALICE: No, I didn't know then. But I recognised him straight away the next time I saw him, at the croquet.

KING: And you saw him take the tarts.

ALICE: Yes, and then he saw me and he said if I told anyone he'd kill me.

The courtroom gasps.

KING: That he'd kill you.

ALICE: Yes.

The courtroom gasps.

KING: This man here?

ALICE: Yes.

KING: I rest my case.

QUEEN: Case closed. Off with his head!

KNAVE: But I haven't asked any questions –

QUEEN: I'm bored now.

KNAVE: Your majesty, please. One last thing before I say goodbye to my head.

QUEEN: Go on then.

The KNAVE comes out from behind his barrier.

KNAVE: Ladies and gentlemen of the jury, permit me to introduce a new piece of evidence.

The KNAVE takes a folded piece of paper out of his pocket.

This was found in Alice's pocket. I think you'll agree it's very. Enlightening.

ALICE feels her pocket – it's now empty.

ALICE: But how did you –

KNAVE: *(Reading.)*
Twas brillig and the slithy toves
Did gyre and gimble in the wabe:
All mimsy were the borogoves,
And the mome raths outgrabe...

ALICE: It's just a silly poem.

KNAVE: I think not.

Beware the Jabberwock, my son!
The jaws that bite, the claws that catch –

Jaws that bite what, may I ask? Claws that catch tarts?

I think it's pretty clear this is a document written by
someone plotting a tart theft –

ALICE: I didn't write it.

KNAVE: *Borogoves* we know to be a slang word young people
use for certain jam-filled foodstuffs –

ALICE: It doesn't mean that. Borogoves are birds with long
legs and feathers all sticking out –

The jury laughs.

It's true, Humpty Dumpty told me! Ask Humpty Dumpty
if you don't believe me.

KING: Perhaps we should call Humpty Dumpty.

The WHITE RABBIT whispers in the KING's ear.

Ah. Shame.

QUEEN: What is it?

KING: Humpty Dumpty had something of a fall. Cavalry
couldn't get there in time.

QUEEN: Carry on, Knave. I'm quite enjoying this.

KNAVE:
So rested he by the Tumtum tree –

Tumtum of course signifying hunger.

And as in uffish thought he stood –

ALICE: I don't know what any of it means.

KNAVE: A brilliant piece of lyrical styling, but the arrogant
criminal always makes one mistake.

Do the jury know, I wonder, what the French for *Jabberwock*
is?

ALICE: The French?

KNAVE: The French for *Jabberwock* is 'Aistolthatartez'.

The crowd gasps.

ALICE: It's just a piece of paper, I didn't write it. Someone sent it to me.

KNAVE: I mean I think the word 'snicker-snack' says it all, don't you?

QUEEN: Guilty!

ALICE: No! It's not fair!

The whole courtroom starts to laugh.

What? What's funny?

QUEEN: Fair? Whoever expected a trial to be fair?

KNAVE: 'It's not fair'!

ALICE: Of course they're supposed to be fair, that's the point.

That's why you have a jury.

KING: What a trial has to do with fairness –

QUEEN: 'It's not fair'! Hilarious!

The QUEEN wipes her eyes.

Oh that's cheered me up.

KNAVE: You're going down! You're going down!

ALICE: But I didn't do anything!

KNAVE: 'It's not fair'!

ALICE: No, shut up and listen. I didn't do anything. He's lying. This is a ridiculous place.

QUEEN: Poor thing thinks life should be fair.

ALICE: You're all idiots. What a stupid bunch of –

The courtroom dissolves in a deluge of bouncing coloured rain.

WHITE RABBIT: Hold on to me.

ALICE holds the WHITE RABBIT's arm until the deluge subsides and the courtroom, and all the people in it, have disappeared.

ALICE lets go of the WHITE RABBIT's arm and backs away from him. They're in a blank space, as when she first met him. ALICE tries to work out what's going on.

WHITE RABBIT: There we go. I think it's –

He looks up. One more drop falls and bounces.

Hmm.

He looks up again. Nothing.

Yes I think it's stopped.

ALICE: So what, are you going to take me to some bonkers jail now? Entomb me in jelly or something?

WHITE RABBIT: Eek. You're angry.

ALICE: I'm furious. That was total nonsense, call that a fair trial –

WHITE RABBIT: It's actually good if you're angry.

ALICE: Is it?

WHITE RABBIT: To be in contact with your – yes – absolutely. Result.

ALICE: What?

WHITE RABBIT: You've found it. You've found your heart.

ALICE looks at him, stunned.

What?

ALICE: *My* heart?

WHITE RABBIT: Yes. Hurrah. I mean – sort of – Go right to the heart, I said.

ALICE: The Heart I was looking for was *my* heart?

WHITE RABBIT: Yes. Bingo. Game over.

ALICE: All this time I'm walking around like a human thesaurus – did he mean the *centre*, or the Heart of the *matter*, or the queen of Hearts or – all this time you just meant *my* heart?

You could have saved me a lot of –

WHITE RABBIT: Yeah but you needed to – to get there on your own. I did say that.

ALICE: I was at a funeral, yeah? That was important, that was –

WHITE RABBIT: This was important.

ALICE: Wandering around flipping Monkey Island talking to one flipping nutter after another?

WHITE RABBIT: To teach you something, help you learn something.

ALICE: Croquet? Tea parties?

WHITE RABBIT: Well the tea party of course was a lesson about time.

ALICE: It was mostly some guff about jam, wasn't it?

WHITE RABBIT: You see what happens is, all the time you're there thinking it's mostly about jam – on the surface, yes – but there's this other voice going into your head sideways telling you time's a great healer, for example, that things'll get better with time and in your heart you know that clocks and time and people all have to move forward, don't they?

ALICE: Obvious.

WHITE RABBIT: There were lessons here for – for you to learn from.

ALICE: What, lessons like steer clear of duchesses, they're all nuts?

WHITE RABBIT: You don't know what life's going to throw at you next.

ALICE: Sometimes life throws you a pig dressed as a baby.

WHITE RABBIT: And you catch it, don't you? You caught it. Set it free.

ALICE: And then a cat-man comes along and does creepy smiling at you.

WHITE RABBIT: Other people's smiles look strange at the moment 'cause you don't feel like smiling yourself.

ALICE: And what about Humpty Dumpty? – he was *horrible.*

WHITE RABBIT: He was difficult. But things have to be difficult sometimes.

Difficult's good for you in the end.

ALICE: And the stupid poem – the Jabberwocky?

WHITE RABBIT: Well that's about your fear of not understanding things. Remember what the Cheshire Cat said about how things don't always make sense? That sometimes you just have to accept it?

ALICE: I hate things that don't make sense.

WHITE RABBIT: But things that don't make sense are as much part of life as things that fit together perfectly. It's your age – you think everything should add up and everything should be fair –

ALICE: Oh don't tell me what a *child* I am.

WHITE RABBIT: I know, I know. You feel a hundred years old.

The thing is that there are some things in the world that can't be understood.

It's time for you to get out of the house, Alice.

ALICE: Don't tell me what I – This was a stupid wild goose chase. God's sake I know exactly where my heart is cause it aches like a –

WHITE RABBIT: Like walking around with a tin bath strapped to your back?

ALICE: He's been dead two weeks and you want me to be dancing around?

WHITE RABBIT: No no, not now – but one day.

Like with Tweedledum and Tweedledee. One day you'll be like them, you'll be able to look back and think about Joe happily, remembering happy things.

Because it's OK to be happy, eventually. And it's OK to laugh, cause Joe would want that, wouldn't he? You mustn't hold yourself back because you think you ought to be in constant pain and if you're not you're being disloyal. And it's OK to eat because you're still –

You mustn't be embarrassed that you're still alive, you know.

ALICE: And what, if I remember all this stuff I'm going to be OK about Joe being dead, am I?

WHITE RABBIT: Oh no. No, that'll take years. We're just working on getting you out of the house.

Remember what the caterpillar said – one day at a time.

ALICE: That's just a stupid cliché.

WHITE RABBIT: It's a cliché because it's true.

Oh, I've got something to give back.

He starts to go through his pockets.

ALICE: What is it?

WHITE RABBIT: No, that's a receipt for some carrots –

Here we are. One plectrum. Compliments of the Wonderland State Border Control.

He hands the plectrum back to ALICE. She looks at it in her hand.

He's always with you.

ALICE puts the plectrum back in her pocket.

ALICE: I feel like a dick.

WHITE RABBIT: Don't feel like a dick. Why d'you feel like a dick?

ALICE: Cause I should have been able to work it out by myself.

WHITE RABBIT: Don't underestimate your brain's ability to fool you, throw you a curve ball. You know, you're going through something massive, something that'd be massively difficult for anyone, and you're only 12.

ALICE: Yeah, let's not get back onto me being 12 again, it –

Wait – my *brain*? What d'you mean, my brain?

WHITE RABBIT: Your brain made Wonderland. For you to hide in for a bit.

ALICE: I made this?

WHITE RABBIT :Which makes you sort of brilliant. Very brilliant, actually.

The WHITE RABBIT goes over to a large wooden box, the same as the one he climbed into at the start.

ALICE: Are you going?

WHITE RABBIT: Your mum and dad are going to need you.

The WHITE RABBIT starts to unpack the box, revealing the armchair from ALICE's living room.

ALICE: My mum hates me.

WHITE RABBIT: Not true.

ALICE: She'd rather have the Knave of Hearts – I mean no – I mean she'd rather have Joe – agh, you've confused me, I can't separate –

WHITE RABBIT: Grown ups aren't always logical either.

ALICE: Everyone's mental.

WHITE RABBIT: Some of the time.

ALICE: Obvious again.

WHITE RABBIT: It's both. It's completely obvious and utterly bewildering. So you do what you can, when you can, and everyone muddles through and just occasionally something's so beautiful it takes your breath away.

ALICE'S DAD's head appears out of the seat of the armchair.

DAD: Hello love.

(Calling.) Suzanne – Suze, she's here, I've found her.

He starts to climb out of the armchair. The WHITE RABBIT backs off, gradually leaves.

Where've you been love, we've been looking everywhere.

ALICE: I've been here.

DAD: Looked everywhere for you.

MUM's head appears through the armchair.

MUM: You're here!

What the bloody hell are you doing, we've been –

DAD: Suze –

MUM: Sorry. Sorry. Graham can you –

DAD helps MUM to climb through the armchair. Both of them stand looking at ALICE.

We were really worried. Thought you'd gone.

DAD: But you've not, so that's good, so –

MUM: The gannets have all gone now, it's just us.

DAD: We should call Helen, tell her to stop looking.

MUM: Auntie Helen's gone out kerbcrawling, looking for you.

MUM looks at ALICE. ALICE looks at the floor.

MUM looks at DAD. He nods.

Your, um. Your dad's pointed out to me that I might not have seemed very nice to you the past few days and I wanted to say I'm –

ALICE: I'm sorry Joe's gone.

MUM: Oh love, of course you are. I know you are. You didn't think I thought you weren't, did you?

ALICE: I don't know.

MUM: Oh petal, come here.

ALICE goes towards her MUM. They falter at about a metre from each other.

MUM touches ALICE's hair.

I'm sorry, love. Sorry I'm so –

I'm not cross with you, petal.

I'm still your mummy.

DAD: We could have a cup of tea if you like. If you're not completely sick of tea today.

ALICE: What d'you mean?

DAD: All that tea we had to drink at the funeral.

ALICE: I'd like a cup of tea.

DAD: Oh but we're out of milk.

MUM: Bloody Helen –

DAD: Love –

MUM: Well she makes it so milky!

DAD: I'll go to Somerfield.

ALICE: I'll get it.

DAD: Pardon?

ALICE: I'll go to the shop and get it.

DAD: OK?

ALICE: Be good for me to get out the house, maybe.

ALICE looks at her MUM, who nods bravely.

Get some fresh air.

MUM: Yes, OK.

DAD reaches in his pocket and pulls out a fiver. ALICE takes it.

ALICE: Thanks. See you in a minute.

ALICE goes. MUM and DAD look at each other. MUM tries not to say something, but after a moment blurts it out:

MUM: *(Calling after her.)* Be careful on the road!

Alice?

They spring into action.

DAD: Watch her out the window...

MUM: Just peek round the curtain so she doesn't see you. What's she doing?

DAD: Hang on a sec, she's not there yet. No, she's coming out the front door –

MUM: Yeah?

DAD: She's walking down to the gate.

She's standing at the gate.

MUM: Is she alright?

DAD: Looks like she's not sure about it –

MUM: Oh heck.

DAD: Hesitating...

MUM goes to the other window.

Don't let her see you, just peek round the curtain.

MUM: She's going – is she going?

DAD: That's it Alice. That's my girl.

MUM and DAD fade away as ALICE comes through the garden gate and onto the pavement.

She breathes deeply. She enjoys the feeling. She starts to walk down the road.

A crowd of WONDERLANDERS appears behind her, including the WONDERBAND. They play music as they follow her. A mash-up of Joe's song with Welcome To Wonderland and the Lobster Quadrille.

ALICE doesn't dance, but the WONDERLANDERS do.

ALICE smiles, knowing they're behind her.

THE END.